Aisle Be Damned

Swaying hips, praying lips & flying tips

National Bestseller
2nd Edition

Rishi Piparaiya

JAICO PUBLISHING HOUSE

Ahmedabad Bangalore Chennai
Delhi Hyderabad Kolkata Mumbai

Published by Jaico Publishing House
A-2 Jash Chambers, 7-A Sir Phirozshah Mehta Road
Fort, Mumbai - 400 001
jaicopub@jaicobooks.com
www.jaicobooks.com

AISLE BE DAMNED
ISBN 978-81-8495-465-4

First Jaico Impression: 2013
Sixth Jaico Impression (Second Edition): 2016
Seventh Jaico Impression: 2018

Cover Images by Madhur Shroff

Page design and layouts: Special Effects, Mumbai

Printed by
Trinity Academy For Corporate Training Limited, Mumbai

MOST OF THE READERS WERE DEFINITELY HIGH!

...outrageously hilarious book.

–Rediff.com

Flying high on wings of humour.

–Deccan Chronicle

I began it with grave reservations, which melted within moments, making me smile at first, and then laugh out loud. It lightened up my mood, and surprisingly soon, too!

–Anuradha Shankar, blogger, A Wandering Mind, anushankarn.blogspot.in

Rishi Piparaiya has truly outdone himself and has shown himself to be a master of satire... Seriously who would have thought that my missing jacket was actually stolen by the Italian mafia.

–Rupertt Wind, blogger, pagesofflife.blogspot.com

...Piparaiya makes the book immensely personal and that is what is most enjoyable about it. The anecdotes will leave you in splits.

–Vivek Tejuja, blogger, thehungryreader.wordpress.com

...very few works make it to the bestseller list in humour and I must say Rishi Piparaiya has raised the bar to the coveted 38,000 feet with his debut venture.

–Priyanka Roy Banerjee, book critic and blogger, TheTalesPensieve.com

The author has an excellent command over the language and coupled with his amazing sense of humour this book is a laugh riot...has taken a mundane topic and created a fabulous book out of that.

–Anjana Avinash, book critic and blogger,
The Greedy Reader, Iamagreedyreader.wordpress.com

... nothing that you thought it to be, and everything that you never guessed it would be. It is fun, humorous, unique, and oh-so- different.

–Amrit Sinha, Goodreads.com

...simply a great book, delivering what it promises and delivering it with consistency.

–Bookgeeks.in

The book is a joyride...in the air...midst of clouds... Oh! I am seriously in love with this book.

–Satya, blogger, Locomente, locomente.blogspot.in

Who said corporate executives don't have a sense of humour, the author has proved them all wrong with a vengeance.

–Venkatarangan, venkatarangan.com Blog

The book is guaranteed to make you think, smile and also roll with laughter every few seconds.

–Amit Rawat, book critic, Pune

You know what worked for the book? We've all been there, done that. And we identify with the tone. The massive heaps of sarcastic dung-bombs that the author is letting fly are actually like a catharsis for our pent- up emotions.

–Reviewed by Vaultofbooks.com

AND THEN THERE WERE SOME WHO WERE SOBER...

I don't remember reading a more childish book than this... If you have taken a few flights in your life – you would have more insights and maybe imagination than the author.

The most useless book I have ever read.

I guess I'm not the target audience.

Couple of anecdotes are interesting but you can't write an entire book of such inane stuff.

**from reviews at Goodreads.com and online bookstores*

This is for you, Rishi

ABOUT THIS SECOND EDITION

Having sold a few more copies than expected, my publishers called me frantically, "Hey, we don't know what's going on with your utterly random book, but it has flown off [pun intended] the shelves and we want to re-launch it. Can you add some content and also give it a global flavor so we can palm it off as a new and international edition?"

Now unlike the other two influential constituents in my life, namely time and tide, my publishers have a predisposition towards waiting. So I focused on more critical tasks at hand, such as scheduling my manicures and pedicures for the rest of the year. But after months of admiring my perfectly finished nails, I couldn't justify procrastinating any longer. So I pulled out my laptop, tapped and tapped, and here I am, thrilled to introduce the second edition of *Aisle Be Damned.*

So what exactly is new? Well, to beef up what is otherwise a deceptively quick read, I have added some additional content, including throwing all caution to the winds, my very intimate experience of a mile-high threesome (blush). I have shared some testimonials from readers of *Aisle Be Damned* – very likely the outcome of their excessive consumption of hallucinogenic substances – but nonetheless gratifying. And I am also tweaking the cover a tad and the aforesaid patient publishers have very kindly slapped on a 'National Bestseller' tag on it.

For international readers, I haven't really made many changes. Flying is pretty much the same the world over and I am sure you will totally get my drift. I do appreciate that citizens of Antarctica may not identify with some of the subject matter, as I don't really cover seaplanes and frigid weather aviation. But that is a demographic segment that I have reluctantly, but consciously, relinquished. For those still confused, I have enlisted the help of my fellow Indians – there are a billion of us levitating around every corner of the world – just grab them by the *lungi* and seek clarifications – they love to talk. They will proudly explain the context behind my writing and then add on a few of their personal anecdotes as well. And finally, if, try as you might, you don't understand the Indian accent and sideward head movements, reach out to my buddy, Googs. He maintains a blog at www.google.com and he will respond to your queries with lightning speed; he is so alert and helpful and I am thrilled to have him as my bestie.

For those who haven't read this book, Congratulations! You are getting a lot more paisa vasool value than the impatient early adopters who had picked up the first edition. And for those who have already read the original, thank you for being curious enough to pick this up anyway. And now that you have, why don't you just trundle over to the cashier and buy it - two *Aisle Be Damned*s will look even better on your bookshelf than just one.

Happy reading and safe, fun travels always!

– Rishi Piparaiya
Mumbai, India
October 2015

THE ESSENTIAL PACKING LIST

For a safe and pleasant journey, please ensure that you have packed the following in your hand baggage. Over the course of the book, you will appreciate why.

1. Machine oil, or any other lubricant
2. A designer jacket
3. A hood that covers your face
4. A sack of birdseed
5. A water bottle
6. A parachute
7. A spare wheel, jack and jumper cables
8. A pad or any protective cushioning for your chin
9. A masala dabba (spice box)
10. A hip flask with a few shots of brandy
11. A stink bomb, or some smelly blue cheese
12. A smartphone or tablet

CONTENTS

INTRODUCTION

Ever since Orville and Wilbur Wright stopped bemoaning their peculiar names and diverted their energies to propelling a heavier-than-air machine, man has been captivated by flight. There is something innately fascinating about these powerful crafts that take off to the sky to the beat of jet engines.

Add to that the glamour that has usually been associated with flying. Smart pilots and flight attendants strutting through terminals as hundreds of eyes enviously follow them. Wild partying in airport hotels, fueled by topsy-turvy hormones from their incessant crisscrossing of time zones. Well-dressed passengers, free flowing alcohol, fine cuisine, dreamy magazines, exotic destinations – air travel has traditionally come with more than its share of flamboyance, ostentation and romance.

In reality, for most of us, taking a flight means hours of boredom, punctuated by moments of stark terror. It starts with a painful drive to the airport and ends with getting fleeced by a crooked cab driver upon landing. And in between, one goes through the sheer drudgery of crowded airports, stiff security, delayed flights, uncomfortable seats, turbulent journeys and lost luggage.

I have probably taken over a thousand flights, each one with a sense of trepidation. For someone who considers the London Eye to be as blood curdling a ride as the nerves can take, blasting through the skies in a pretty metal tube is certainly not top priority. But professional responsibilities, as well as personal desires to explore a world beyond 19°N 73°E, require that I go to the airport a few times a week for the dog and pony show of air travel.

This book is the accumulated knowledge of the tens of thousands of hours that I have logged in flights, airports, immigration counters, baggage carousels and the like. Nuggets of wisdom that I hope will maximize your flying experience and help you soar through safer, friendlier and more enjoyable skies.

Happy reading and safe travels.

IT ALL BEGINS AT THE AIRPORT

"It can hardly be a coincidence that no language on earth has ever produced the expression, 'As pretty as an airport'."
— Douglas Adams, *The Long Dark Tea-time of the Soul*

You need to go back about a hundred years in history to understand the origin of airports. A couple of pilgrims managed to escape from Hell, took the wrong trapdoor back to the earth's surface and somehow happened to find themselves seated on bar stools next to an architect in Guam. Over pitchers of US island-territory tipple, they described to him the horrors of the convoluted labyrinths, urine-filled cesspools, skeleton figurines and indigenous insect species. The Guamanian architect made furious sketches as they ubble-gubbled on in animated terror. And based on that chance encounter was born the first design of the modern airport.

The monotony of flight starts here. Can there be anything drearier than tall facades of glass and concrete staring down unwelcomingly? Glittering digital screens flashing 'Flight Delayed' in multiple languages, serpentine queues, weary travelers, badly labeled luggage, frayed tempers, artificial plants – airports have them all.

BAGGAGE TROLLEYS

Your airport experience starts with the hunt for a trolley to load your luggage on. These are usually grouped, one interlinked with the other, in trolley stands around the airport. Incidentally, they were designed by the petite mistress of the aforesaid architect, who constructed the interlocking levers such that one could not detach just a single trolley from the stack. You struggle with the trolley handle, alternately exercising vigorous pushing and pulling motions, but the damn thing just doesn't come loose. After a couple of attempts you give up, look around sheepishly and request someone to hold the rest of the trolleys while you jerk one out.

Trolleys follow a random Brownian motion as you push them along, so expect the journey to take longer than planned. *One* of the wheels, of *one* of the trolleys, in *one* of the trolley stands, in *one* of the terminals of the airport, wobbles with *one* of the most excruciating sounds at the upper end of man's auditory threshold. Congratulations and you are the lucky winner! You have won the fantastic opportunity to attract the annoyed attention of every person within a fifty-meter radius as you trundle your way to the check-in desk.

Though you can ignore it – just look down and keep pushing – the problem is easily addressed. Clean the dust, dirt and debris around the offending wheel and pull out the bottle of machine oil (item 1 in your essential packing list) from your carry-on bag. Apply a generous amount and that should fix it.

CHECK-IN AND BUSINESS CLASS UPGRADES

I have never really understood check-in. What a bizarre process this is – one stands in a long check-in queue to collect a boarding card, and then one stands in a boarding queue sixty minutes later to hand it over? It just doesn't make sense.

There is no upside to check-in. In most countries, check-in is the point where you pay additional fees for every conceivable service that the airline can think of: extra baggage, window seat, oxygen, and so forth. Some airlines, however, have not gone down this mercenary route – they rip-off passengers in the base airfare itself. In such situations, there can be only one positive outcome to the check-in process – a complimentary upgrade to business class. So let's focus on that.

To occupy business class, one needs to look like the business class. So dress well, at least above the waist, which is the section of your body that is visible to the check-in attendant. It doesn't matter if you are wearing shorts, tracks or even just your underwear south of the equator. But ensure that your upper body sports a well-tailored shirt and nice jacket.

Choose the check-in attendant carefully. If you are male, attractive young female attendants are to be avoided – they distract you into making frivolous conversation, have little authority to determine upgrades and are primarily focused on their phones as they check you in. Also avoid male check-in attendants. They are generally envious and would rather be on the flight and in your seat rather than checking you in. It is not about you; it is just a male-to-male thing. You need to find the most stately lady in the vicinity: someone with a dash of gray, a posture that screams authority and a calm demeanor that indicates years of experience in determining who is and who is not upgrade-worthy.

Flash her a beaming smile, and as you glance at her name badge, address her by first name thus, *"Good Morning Janet. I am flying to Delhi."* Wait as she taps the various keypads and scans the screens. If you see her proceeding to print a standard economy boarding card, ask her, *"Janet, so is it a full flight this morning? Any possibility you might upgrade me to business?"* At this point, flip your jacket open with a loud *"Damn, it's so hot in here,"* so that she looks up and sees a luxury designer label on the inside pocket.

Also keep a bottle of any ultra-fancy water brand accessible, have an elegant swig and then slam it with a refreshing sigh on the counter. Ensure that it's not one of those small complimentary bottles that you could have conceivably swiped from a hotel minibar.

Nor should it be a humongous one-liter monstrosity that you obviously purchased to profit from some economies of scale. No sir. There's something about a person who travels with a compact 500 ml bottle of it's-more-expensive-than-champagne water that just screams Business Class. And it's not like you actually have to buy it every time you travel – I just keep re-filling, from the kitchen tap, the sole bottle of Evian that I purchased in 2009.

Janet might upgrade you or she might not. In some cases, she might even put you on a wait list and ask you to check at the gate before boarding. If you're relegated to the last of these instances, please refer to the gate-upgrade strategy in the following chapter.

Airline check-in staff can be divided into shoddy upgraders and classy upgraders. A shoddy upgrader waits for you to request an upgrade, hems and haws, checks with her supervisor and then with a sigh, prints the upgraded business class boarding pass and hands it over. A classy upgrader flashes you a smile from the minute she spots the bespoke sports coat. She doesn't ask questions and doesn't make small conversation; she efficiently taps keys, prints and attaches luggage tags and hands over the boarding card with a *"Have a pleasant flight, sir."*

As you walk away from the desk, marveling at her efficiency, you glance at the card and see a seat number in the low single digits – an upgrade to business class without you having to ask or her having to mention. You turn in slow motion and whisper, *"Thank You."* And she places her right palm on her heart, tilts her head a couple of degrees and mouths, *"You are welcome."*

It's a pleasure to deal with classy upgraders. Sadly, the more classy upgraders an airline has, the faster it seems to file for bankruptcy.

"Sir, we ask you for the last time: do you or do you not have a metal coin in your pocket?"

SECURITY CHECK

Piparaiya is surely a nefarious organization in some part of the world because invariably, as I cross the metal detector, lights flash, buzzers beep and officers start hissing *"Code Red, Code Red"* in their walkie-talkies. I am whisked away to a corner and made to straddle split while they run a hand-held detector all over me, rip apart my bags and bounce my laptop to ensure that it is genuine.

To efficiently get through the full monty, start preparing for the security check once there are about six people ahead of you in the queue. That's just about how much time you need to loosen your belt, slip off your jacket, pull out your laptop and dump the phones and BlackBerrys into the plastic tray.

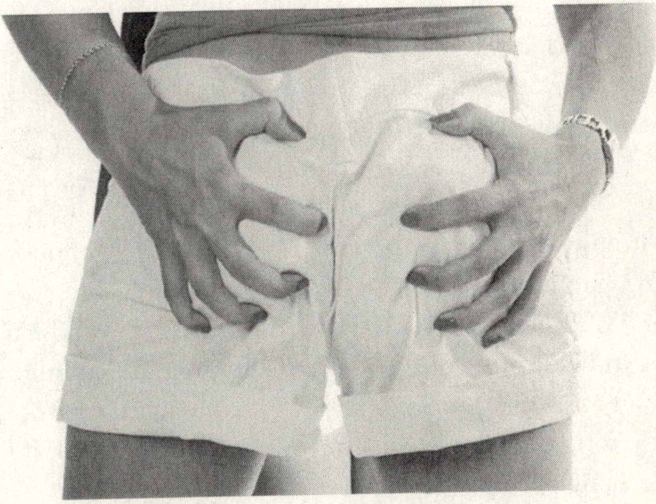

"Just another month of this boring job and I should get promoted as a supervisor on the X-ray machines."

As Ryan Bingham (George Clooney) in the must-watch movie *Up in the Air* advised, *"Never get behind old people. Their bodies are littered with hidden metal and they never seem to appreciate how little time they have left. Bingo, Asians. They pack light, travel efficiently and they have a thing for slip-on shoes. Gotta love 'em."*

Start raising your arms as you walk through the metal detector toward the security guard on the other side. Stiffen up completely as he pats your ass. Yell *"What the shit!"* if it continues for over ten seconds.

Throw up your arms if your bag gets pulled out of the X-ray machine for a further check. Unzip the bag with a look of sheer disgust, repeatedly checking your watch, as if it's the security official alone who is standing between you and a plane full of impatient passengers. And then look away when he pulls out nail-cutters, water bottles, scissors and batteries from your bag.

The above routine can get disrupted if a gaggle of pilots and cabin crew show up just as you are reaching the end of the queue. Pilots and crew members would like us to believe they have precedence over the common man at security queues. They will barge in at the front, avoiding eye contact with anyone, and assume that it is their right. *Wrong!*

Tap them on the shoulder, look them in the eye, snap your fingers and say, *"Get back, buddies."* If they still don't listen, stamp your foot on their shiny, black shoes. If they continue to be difficult, get them to circle around you, and with your lightning-fast karate maneuver, go clockwise kneeing each of them in the nuts and body slamming them to the floor. The audacious buggers!

"Sayonara, punk!"

OTHER ASPECTS OF AIRPORTS

An outstanding spot in airport lounges is standing out, spotting people trying to get in. They start by proffering their boarding card – *"Of course I know I am not flying business, but don't you know that I am a privileged member?"* That is obviously not the case according to the human iPad seated at the desk.

They then make the Wallet move. They pull out a stash of credit cards and place them with a flourish on the desk, as if they are pocket aces that have just won them the World Poker Championship.

"Can I get entry if I have a MasterCard?"

"No."

"Visa?"

"No."

"American Express?"

"No."

"Debit card?"

"No."

"Visiting card?"

"No."

"Christmas card?"

"No!"

Having unsuccessfully tested all possible rectangular credentials including their SIM card, they mutter a cuss word, look as if the greatest travesty possible has been inflicted on them and walk away from that traveler's heaven in a huff.

Control your schadenfreude and wait for the next dummy.

What is it with banks and their fascination for aerobridges? Pick any airport in any country and you will find the logo of some bank, in 300-point geriatric font, adorning the insides and outsides of aerobridges. And while most banks are struggling with government bailouts and financial scams, some are still managing to offer great deals to consumers. I lately came across aerobridge advertisements offering up to a 50% return. For every $100 that you invest with them, they will return as much as half when you retire.

Many airports have moving walkways – escalators along the ground – that save passengers a trek to their gate. So what kind of walkway user are you?

- Walkway Standers: People who really need to conserve energy. They can be identified by their strict adherence to instructions such as 'Hold the Railings' and 'Watch Your Step' as well as by a keen interest in hoardings advertising knee and hip replacements.

- Walkway Walkers: People in a rush. They walk or jog on moving walkways, thereby significantly increasing their velocity. Any time gained though is invariably lost when stumbling off the walkway as it comes to an end.

- Walkway Lovers: Couples standing side by side treating the sojourn as the mechanical equivalent of a romantic stroll in Central Park. They are usually spotted with a trail of irritable Walkway Walkers fidgeting behind them.

- Walkway Terrors: Little kids who consider this to be the airport equivalent of Disney's 'It's a Small World' ride. They barrel down the walkways in the opposite direction, tripping the walkers, shoving the standers and breaking up the lovers.

As for me, I believe that the ground should only move in the event of an earthquake. I therefore prefer to walk my way.

Years after the SARS and bird flu scares, I still see some hypochondriacs walking around airports wearing surgical face-masks. Actually, we can't blame them: airports are densely polluted with germs, bacteria and viruses, the cause of common colds and similar ailments. And in any case, it's not as if they are wearing them all the time. Why, many of them remove the masks every half hour in the smoking rooms, as they light up their next cancer stick.

Only One in Seven: Go to any of those mobile recharge stations that dot most airport terminals. You know what I am talking about right? Those kiosks with a variety of phone chargers, of all popular makes and models, where one can plug in a phone for some last minute juice before takeoff.

Only one in every seven of those chargers is operational. Naturally, a dude has already found it and is standing there stoically till his battery goes all the way from zero to 100%. The other six wires are utterly useless. At best you can use them to strangle yourself in frustration.

Here's a real fun game to play if you have 15 minutes to kill. Take 50 dollars to any currency exchange counter and convert it to the local currency. Then take the local currency to the adjacent counter and convert it back to dollars. Then return to the original counter and convert what you have back to the local currency. Keep track of how many transactions it takes for you to be left with no money.

Seven and below: Beep. Try again.

Eight and above: Ding, Ding, Ding, Ding! Awesome job!

Screw the shops; I want a duty-free office.

THE OPTIMAL BOARDING STRATEGY

"What does it mean to pre-board?
Do you get on before you get on?"
— George Carlin

The optimal boarding strategy is dependent on your answers to the following questions.

- Are you flying business class?
- Are you flying economy class?
- Are you flying first class?
- Are you hoping for a last minute upgrade at the boarding gate?
- Are you going to be doing the 'Walk of Shame'?

FLYING BUSINESS

If you are flying business, it is best to board as early as possible. Most airlines have a separate boarding queue for business passengers, so you should strut ahead, flash your boarding card and clamber onto your spacious reclining seat.

Once at your seat, adopt the Business Class Posture (BCP). The BCP has been refined over the years by business-class travellers to elicit maximum awe and envy from hoi polloi who are trekking to economy.

Essentially, the posture requires that you put your boarding card on the armrest, where it is visible to gapers who can read it and register your celebrity status. The posture involves taking sophisticated sips of a beverage at regular intervals. And it requires you to dive into any newspaper that you find, keeping one eye sharply cocked to gauge the reactions of passersby.

FLYING ECONOMY

Surprisingly, the boarding strategy doesn't change even if you are flying economy. Start by boarding early to snag valuable baggage space in the overhead bins. Then grab the nice newspapers and magazines that are stuffed in the business-class seat pockets – this is easier to do when the seats are unoccupied. Lastly, attendants are usually up and about, serving refreshing juices and champagnes to the business-class passengers who have settled in. Grab a glass from their tray and walk on to economy, without skipping a beat.

FLYING FIRST

If you are flying first class and are reading this book, you really need to get a life. Go start a foundation or rid the world of malaria or something. Make yourself useful.

GATE UPGRADES

If your astrologer or psychic had a premonition that you may get upgraded at the gate, wait until the majority of passengers have boarded. By this time, the staff know how many business passengers made last minute cancellations and if economy is full. So hand over your card and wait nervously as the attendant scans it and checks her system. Pings from the machine, a startled expression or a scramble for a pen to write down your new seat number are all good indications that the upgrade has happened.

LAST-MINUTE BOARDING

If you think nobody in this world cares about you, delay boarding your flight. Your name will be announced all over the airport, your mug shot splashed across TV screens and you will have men and women with Wanted posters running around looking for you. *"Paging passenger Piparaiya. This is the last and final call for Rishi Piparaiya."*

I love it! This is the closest to fame that I will ever get.

THE WALK OF SHAME

The 'Walk of Shame' refers to the journey that a passenger, usually accustomed to flying business, makes through the business-class section when he happens to be flying economy.

This phenomenon is typically observed during the years of economic slowdown that follow a sustained period of growth activity. When business is booming, corporate executives fly business class. But this is one of the first perks to go when markets turn. As the economy heads south, so do the executives. Suit-and-tie clad professionals who were once making the difficult choice between hot and cold towels in business are now relegated to rough paper tissues in economy.

If all organizations went through the same crisis at the same time, this might be fine. The shame arises when you run across acquaintances merrily occupying the front section, their HR departments still unable to spell austerity, while you make your way to the back. You slink your way with eyes averted and a hood (item three on your packing list) across your mortified face, as they do the BCP on the very seat that you used to occupy in the good old days of double-digit growth.

The only people who never have to do the walk of shame are investment bankers and private equity folks. It's a wonder that airlines don't dedicate specific seats to them, the way it's done with benches in parks and promenades. They can be identified by their uniforms (light blue shirt, dark grey trousers, yellow tie if investment banking and no tie if private equity). If they are on holiday, it's a white cotton shirt and jeans. And all of them have flat stomachs, rimless glasses and a chronic addiction to fruit platters.

The rest of the corporate world, at one time or another, faces the ultimate stigma – the walk of shame. And the only way to avoid it is to be the first to board, before anyone else. If possible, even before the cabin or the cleaning crew. Just board and hope that you can drown unnoticed in a capful of bottled airline water.

"I am in seat 2-Bain Capital. You? Seat 5-Goldman Sachs? Dude, that's way behind!"

THERE'S A BUS?

It is pertinent to note that these rules only apply when boarding via aerobridges. If you are taking a bus, as could be the case in regional airports, it impacts the entire boarding strategy. To understand how, let me introduce two key accounting and data processing principles: FIFO and LIFO.

In a FIFO (First In, First Out) system, the first items entered are the first ones to be taken out. Imagine a tollbooth where cars from all over enter the toll lane and head to the booth to pay the toll. Each car pays the toll and heads out in the same sequence in which it entered the toll lane, and this is the FIFO method.

LIFO (Last In, First Out) is the opposite of FIFO and here, the last items entered are the first to be removed. Imagine taking an empty jar and filling it up with cookies. Once it is filled to the top you start removing cookies, one at a time. The last cookies that were placed in the jar are the first ones to be removed. This is the LIFO method.

So if you are boarding a plane via an aerobridge, you are first through the boarding gate and first onto the plane. First in, First Out: FIFO.

Now here is where it gets complicated. If you are getting into a bus, you suddenly get switched to the

LIFO process. Passengers who board the bus early get pushed into the interiors by those behind them. So the passengers who board later end up near the exit doors and are the first to get off when the bus reaches the plane. Last in the bus, first out of the bus: LIFO. And then you are the first into the plane.

So if you are taking a bus to the plane, you need to adapt. You go through the gate early using FIFO and then hang around the bus, without getting in, so that you can use LIFO. Stumbling on your carry-on bag, bending over to tie shoelaces, or feigning a heart attack are some good ways to fall behind your co-passengers who are boarding the bus.

A couple of flights and you will gain sufficient practice – it sounds more complex than it actually is.

"Okay, this should help me memorize the rule: L for laces, L for LIFO, L for laces, L for LIFO, L for laces . . ."

SHOULD I WINDOW OR SHOULD I AISLE?

"There are only two reasons to sit in the back row of an airplane: either you have diarrhea, or you're anxious to meet people who do."
— Henry Kissinger

Whether you choose the window or the aisle seat (if the center seat has even crossed your mind, you need serious professional help), primarily depends on how much you like clouds. Clouds are complex objects – I consider myself to be reasonably intelligent, but I still find this 'liquid droplets suspended in the atmosphere' concept fascinating. Where is the liquid? Why are clouds white? How is rain appearing magically out of nowhere? And I'm not even getting into snow and hail, which are in a different league of wonder altogether.

Clouds are nice and fluffy. If you like cotton, bunnies or candy floss, you will also like clouds. And if you like clouds, you should sit on the window seat because chances are pretty good, unless you are goddamn unlucky, that you will spot some clouds.

WHEN TO WINDOW

In addition to giving you the opportunity to stare at beautiful clouds, window seats have these advantages.

- ↗ Windows provide a natural headrest. This is of course irrelevant if you are one of those travelers who think nothing of resting their head on a random co-passenger's shoulder.

- They help to prevent mid-air collisions (see chapter *Beyond the Safety Information Card*).

- If you find yourself in a hostage situation, the probability of getting screwed is lower if you're at the window. I mean, put yourself in a terrorist's olive-green combat boots. Would you rather scare the living daylights out of an aisle passenger or would you ask him to move aside, so that the window passenger can step out and be your hostage? I haven't yet had any experience as a hostage, but common sense, validated by Hollywood flicks, dictates that aisle passengers get shafted more during hijacks.

A typical view of the clouds from the window seat

AISLE BE DAMNED!

Now if you don't have a particular fancy for clouds, you could just as well sit in the aisle seat. You will see a lot of armrests and elbows. And strips of floor level lighting that supposedly twinkle in minor emergency situations, such as slamming hard into the ground. From the aisle seats, you can also make a quicker dash to the exits if required. And aisle seats are easier for people with hyperactive bladders. The flip side of course is that your flight is ruined if you are seated next to a perpetual pee-er, dashing back and forth to the loo.

And oh yes, stewards and stewardesses will keep swaying up and down, but well, that is nothing to write home about…

Typical views of armrests and seatbacks from the aisle seat

UGH, THE CENTER

There are absolutely nil, repeat nil, upsides to being in the center seat. Unless by some ginormous twist of fate you are seated between two models, in costume, who are heading to Ibiza for the *Sports Illustrated* swimsuit issue shoot.

Center seats are only occupied by monks, children and duffers who checked in late. Center-seat pockets are the waste buckets for window and aisle passengers, who shove in chewing gum, chocolate wrappers, used diapers, snorted tissues and insect parts when no one is looking. Center-seat occupants deserve sympathy, a pat on the back and any loose change in your wallet.

Even if there are two of you flying together, wanting to sit with each other, do not take a center seat. Take two adjacent aisle seats – one on either side of the aisle. You can talk just as well across the aisle, and even if you are holding hands, you can let go for a few seconds every time the attendants or passengers pass by. Alternatively, take the window and the aisle. Unless there is a group tour of monks on board, chances are that the center seat will remain empty, and you will both have a comfortable flight. And in case some doofus does occupy the center seat, you can exchange your window or aisle with him anyway.

"Great news brothers, it's a full flight. They've got center seats for all of us."

THE MID-SECTION

While window versus aisle is the fundamental seating decision that a traveler needs to make, an almost equally important choice is which section of the plane should one sit in.

The mid-section is the best from all possible perspectives.

- The mid-section of the fuselage, where the wings are attached, is considered to be the strongest. So in the event of a crash from 38,000 feet, guess which section has the best chance of coming out unscathed, without a dent?

- ↗ The food-and-drinks trolley rolls by at just the right time – neither too early, nor too late.
- ↗ You are equidistant from two sets of restrooms – the ones in the front as well as the rear.
- ↗ Back to hijack movies: hostages are usually taken from the front or the rear of the plane. No one really gives a damn about the people in the middle – they are seated there primarily for screaming and fainting.

THE FRONT SECTION

If you can't manage to get a seat in the mid-section, the front is the next best choice, primarily because turbulence is felt the least here. Airflow in the plane is usually from front to back so if you are one of those who prefer fresh oxygenated air to stale warm breath, the closer to the front you are, the better. The downside of being seated in the front is that all howling babies somehow seem to congregate here.

THE REAR SECTION

The rear of the plane is terrible. It bobbles up and down like a yo-yo in the smallest air pockets. The restrooms are constantly wafting out unpleasant odors. Drunken passengers assemble here to discuss gibberish.

The only benefit of being at the rear is that the flight attendants use this section as their home base. So well, if you follow all the tips that I am sharing in this book, you can be assured of a lot of conversations with them during their breaks.

SHOULD I LEFT OR RIGHT?

Once you have chosen your section of the plane, the only open item is which side of the plane should you sit in. The primary factor that influences whether you sit on the left or right side of the plane is whether it's a daytime or nighttime flight.

If it's a daytime flight, you need to remember the first law of the luminaries: the sun rises in the east and sets in the west. And unless you are a sunflower or Vitamin D deprived, I assume you would like to avoid sunlight streaming on your face at 38,000 feet. So if you are flying north in the morning, choose the left side of the plane because the sun will be on the right. And if it's late afternoon, choose the right side because the sun would have moved west, to the left side. Reverse the strategies if you are flying south. If you're flying east or west, I'm not really sure what you should be doing. Please consult your local astronomer.

If it's a nighttime flight, the sun is no longer a factor and moonlight is thankfully not as harsh on the skin. What is a factor, however, is whether you want to nap or not. If you do, you would have chosen a window seat for the natural headrest that it provides. So now all you need to determine is which side your head tilts when you sleep. Some necks go to the right and others to the left. If you are a right side head tilter, choose the window seat on the right side of the plane and vice versa. It's as simple as that.

If you don't plan to sleep, you will probably want to make notes from this book while seated on the aisle seat. So if you're left handed, sit on the left side of the plane and if you're right handed take the right. That will prevent your elbow from jutting out into the aisle as you write – a food trolley hitting an elbow can be mighty painful.

NONE OF THE ABOVE

There is a proposal by a low-cost Irish airline to sell standing-room tickets. Passengers will pay as low as a few pounds to stand their way at the rear of the plane on intercontinental European flights. The last few rows will be removed to create extra space for these standing passengers. They will be given straps to hang onto for support, quite like what you have on buses and trains.

In a related development, a delegation of European

scientists is touring India to study the center of gravity of train travellers. Results from their experiments will not only enhance the experience of standing-room flight passengers back home, but also revolutionize airplane rooftop travel in the Western world.

"Won't see you till Tuesday, man! Flying with the wife for a weekend in Goa – got a sweet deal on hang-from-the-wing tickets."

OTHER ASPECTS OF SEATING

It is heart-wrenching to see people struggling to fit oversize bags into the overhead bins. They push and shove the bags with great force, rotate them upside down and try every possible angle, permutation and combination. But see, here's the deal Einstein – if the volume of your bag is more than the volume of the bin, it just won't fit.

Never put carry-on luggage in overhead bins behind your seat row. It is the biggest blunder that only a doofus could make. As the plane makes its landing approach, most passengers adopt the 'on your marks, get set' pose perfected by athletes starting a track and field race. Leaning forward on the edge of the seat, toes curled and heels raised, waiting for the wheels to touch down – the flight equivalent of the starting gun going off. And over the ineffective *"Please remain seated"* entreaties of the attendants, impatient passengers swamp the aisles in anticipation of the de-boarding dash.

Now in that scenario, imagine trying to weave your way through a 12-inch aisle packed with 40-inch waists, in the reverse direction, to recover a suitcase that is eight rows behind. Forget about it!

Ever seen really large families boarding a flight? A clan comprising the husband, wife, four kids, aunties, uncles and grandparents. They traipse into the plane in ascending height order with the shortest kid leading the way, the grandparents hobbling somewhere in between and the men of the house bringing up the rear. And as they walk into the plane one of them starts bellowing, *"You all can sit anywhere in the 16th to 18th rows. Sit anywhere in the 16th to 18th rows. Anywhere, you get it? Wherever you want. We have booked all three rows. Any seat on row 16, 17 or 18."*

Good job, man! You get a gold star for your immaculate planning.

"From the river in the west to as far as the eye can see to the north, all the land is ours."

Parting can be really difficult, especially when you are a couple so much in love. It's a sinking feeling, letting go of the other's tightly clasped hand, looking at each other with moist eyes, sharing an uncertain farewell kiss and whispering a quavering, *"I will see you when I see you."*

Tough luck, my friends. Check in earlier next time so

that you can get seats next to each other. But for this flight, it is you on your center seat and she on hers.

Only an idiot would not know what triskaidekaphobia is. Thankfully, you are aware that it is the fear of the number 13, which is considered to be a real shit unlucky number. Many airplanes don't have the 13th row. They have the 12th row and then they immediately jump to row 14. But it's not like they have left an empty space where row 13 should have been; they have essentially numbered row 13 as row 14.

Whatever! As if that will confuse the bad luck demons. If your plane has the row 13 and moreover, you are seated on it, you better be freaking triskaidekafied.

I have a hypothesis that center-seat passengers have a significantly lower IQ than those who are on the window or aisle. Maybe it's just a temporary lapse of intellect and they are full-fledged Einsteins on the ground, but I have to admit that I still haven't encountered any center-seat passenger who has impressed me (thus far) with his brainpower. I recently encountered one prime example of this species of intellectually challenged flyers on a Mumbai-Bengaluru flight. I was seated on the window, this dimwit in the center, and an aged gentleman on the aisle. The senior citizen was part of a larger group, and as soon everyone had boarded, he found an empty seat next to his friends and hobbled away as the plane started taxiing. So that left me on the window, ignoramus in the center, and the aisle seat now vacant.

Phew, we shall have some elbow space after all, I thought and turned to the fused bulb with a knowing smile. He looked at the empty aisle seat next to him and smiled back, without making any attempt to move. Maybe he's waiting for the plane to take off, I thought, and waited until we reached cruising altitude and the seat belt signs went off with a "ting". I turned towards him, but he was fast asleep by now, his head lolling against the empty aisle seatback. Resisting the urge to pinch him awake, I turned away impatiently. A while later, the meal service began and the food trolley hunkered by with loud clanging noises. Dumbbell woke up, smacked his lips, glanced yet again at the empty aisle seat next to him, but made no attempt to move.

I was losing it by now. The flight attendants who kept passing by were giving us enquiring looks– as one might to two people, who are not a couple, sitting side by side rather than opposite each other, at a restaurant table. I tapped him on the shoulder. "Excuse me, would you like to move to the adjacent seat so we both have some more space?" And I pointed to the obviously empty seat next to him.

Dingbat stared at me with guppy eyes, his tongue darting between his lips like a reptile. I could almost hear his rusty brain crank itself up during the long pause.

"No, I'm comfortable," he said.

I stared at him. He stared back.

And then with a start, he leaned over and pointed to the seat recline button. "Here, you be comfortable too", he said, pushing an imaginary button in the air with his thumb. If looks could kill, he would have disintegrated into ashes right there and then. Ashes which I would have gladly spread on the empty aisle seat next to him.

ELBOW CHESS

A flight is just a subtle battle for elbow space.

A 16-inch armrest can be divided into two halves. The 8-inch stretch at the rear, which is perpendicular to the backrest, is the good half. Essentially, you can comfortably rest your elbows while you lean against the seatback, which is indeed very nice. The bad half is the front eight inches, where you need to lean forward if you want to prop your elbows. That is not very comfortable.

Therefore, first-mover advantage is critical. As soon as you settle down, firmly glue your elbows to the good half and do not let go for the rest of the flight. Your opponent will try various counter moves such as gently trying to nudge your elbow out with his; or asking you for the newspaper and then grabbing the good half when you reach out for it; or saying that he wants to use the restroom and then occupying the armrest instead as you step out to let him pass. Beware such deceptions.

The biggest dilemma arises during meal service. Do you eat or do you retain your elbow position? Which is why I recommend the aisle or window seat: you can keep one hand firmly planted on the common center-seat armrest and eat using the other.

Look, as with most things in life, speed and agility are important, but at the end of the day, it all boils down to how badly you want to win.

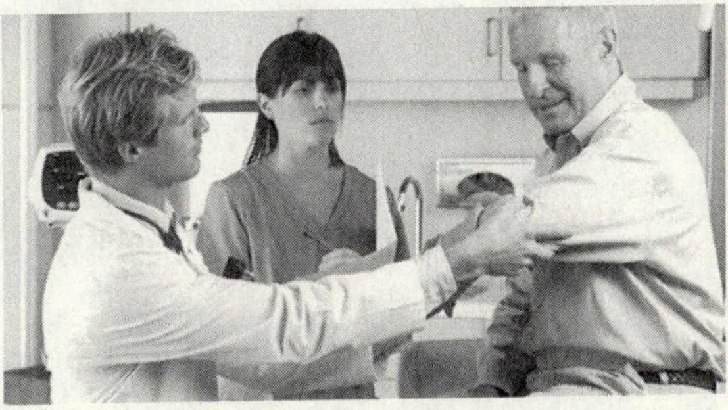

"Yeah, we've been seeing a lot of this lately. Center-seat, were you?"

FLIGHT SAFETY: FROM TAKEOFF TO LANDING

"It's better to be down here wishing you were up there, than up there wishing you were down here."

— Anonymous

Flying is not dangerous. But crashing can be.

According to statisticians, most accidents take place within a few minutes of takeoff or landing, so that's when you need to be most alert. And obviously one should limit the number of landings and takeoffs that one makes. Which means go for non-stop flights rather than multi-route ones, even if the multi-route ones are cheaper, more convenient or the only available option. If the destination is not one flight away, I don't think it is worth visiting.

PRE-TAKEOFF PROCEDURES

Bird strikes are a serious threat to flight safety, but there is a foolproof method of preventing them. As you board, empty the sack of birdseed that you are carrying, thanks to my packing list, through the gap between the aerobridge and the plane. Before someone yells, *"Hey, Stop!"* it should be all over the ground. This move essentially attracts all feathered friends within a five-mile radius to the gate, thereby leaving the surrounding skies clear and free for takeoff.

"This is the Captain. We need about 3,000 pounds of body fat to move to the right of the plane immediately."

Once you have boarded and stashed your luggage, take a walk around the plane. Look at the passengers seated on the left and right and mentally calculate whether the load is balanced. You don't want to be flying tilted at 30 degrees, just because all the whales happen to be seated on one side. Rejig passengers and bags around till you are satisfied with the weight balance.

Read the safety instructions card carefully, say *"hmm"* and keep scratching your chin. This may cause some stress to your co-passengers. And while most people ignore the flight safety demonstration conducted by the cabin crew, ensure that you pay rapt attention. Make eye contact with the stewardess and appear most interested in her pantomime. She will appreciate your interest and be particularly nice to you for the rest of the flight.

Sometimes they race ahead and if you miss something, interrupt with an *"Excuse me, can you repeat that last point you made – about how to blow air through the pipe to inflate the life vest?"* They are usually very happy to oblige.

THE TAKEOFF HURDLE

If your lungs are oxygenated, the seat belt has not been fastened tight enough. Grip the armrests as the plane hurtles down the runway and as it takes off, gauge whether it is at a clean horizontal angle or whether it is tilting. If it is tilting, lean in the opposite direction to help balance out the weight and ask your neighbors to lean as well.

You need to listen for three distinct sounds before relaxing your guard:

- The loud creaking sound of retracting wheels – once the wheels are in, chances of them hitting a stray antenna, treetop, or cow are reduced to virtually nil.

- A ping directed to the cabin crew, which indicates that they can start the cabin service.

- A ping that signals the 'fasten seat belt' sign going off, implying that passengers can roam freely around the cabin.

Alternatively, the pings could simply mean that someone forgot to switch off their BlackBerry messenger.

But well done. You have crossed the takeoff hurdle.

*"I like to Moo-it, Moo-it, I like to Moo-it, Moo-it,
I like to Moo-it, Moo-it, You like ta Moo-it."*

SAFE LANDINGS

There are various things to keep in mind as the plane descends. First, you need to gauge the rate of descent. Is the flight descending at a constant rate or is it plummeting? Plummeting is not a good verb when it comes to flight. Plummeting is bad. If it's plummeting, yell out in the cabin, *"We are plummeting!"* Someone will surely take notice.

If you are seated in an aircraft fitted with cameras, switch to the view from the nose of the plane and observe whether it is aligned with the runway.

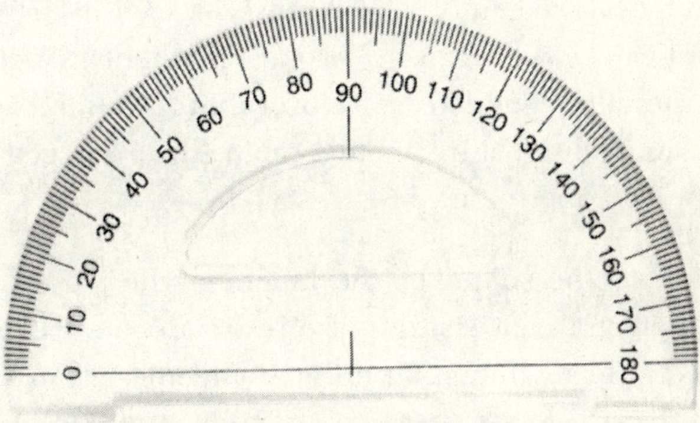

"Ma'am, I think the captain is a few degrees off to the left. Take this and ask him to recheck his coordinates."

Keep your ears cocked for the sound of landing gear getting deployed. It sounds like a bomb going off, so don't get distracted. Wait for the entire whine to reach its end; if the whine stops midway, it means that the gear is stuck and that is ultra-deep trouble.

Heave a sigh of relief when the back wheels touchdown and another for the front wheels. The plane will then hurtle down the runway and you should brace for impact as it could skid, hit a fence or the brakes could fail. As it turns off the main runway, look out for any incoming aircraft. It would be a real pity to have made this whole trip safely only to get roasted in a sideswipe, a few meters from the gate.

MID-FLIGHT VIGILANCE

Don't be lulled into a false sense of security by the statisticians. A lot can go wrong mid-flight as well – engine failure, sudden explosion, cabin decompression, mid-air collision, fire in the cabin, the roof getting ripped off and so on.

Listen to the sound of the engines, which are to a frequent traveler what a pulse is to a doctor. Engines make a steady humming noise. Sometimes when they go through clouds, they seem to groan and that's fine. Sometimes the engines go quiet and that's when you need to panic. Why would the engines just go quiet – has the pilot turned them off to save fuel, as one might do when going downhill in a car? How cheap! If the engines are silent for a long period of time, check with the captain.

"In what has been acclaimed as the biggest development in air safety this century, all seats will now come equipped with water bottles."

Start the water bottle test upon reaching cruising altitude. This is easy to perform, can be done on any airline seat and gives one as much information on relative altitudinal direction as any fancy cockpit instrument.

Pull out item 5, a water bottle, and have a couple of swigs such that the bottle is now three-fourths full. Place it on the tray table and spend the rest of the flight observing the water level.

The water should ideally be still and the level flat; this indicates a smooth and steady flight. If the water tilts forward or backwards, it indicates that the plane is rising or descending and you need to wonder why. If the water tilts to the left or right, it means that the plane is doing the same. If the water churns, it indicates turbulence – the more the churning, the heavier the turbulence. And if the water is churning and tilting, that's disaster in the making.

If you are in a newer airplane with a comprehensive in-flight entertainment console, you are all set. The only entertainment you need is the in-flight moving map system, which gives you valuable information on the aircraft location, distance, altitude, airspeed and local time. You are as empowered as the pilot and can correlate all manual observations with real-time data.

Engine noise should match the airspeed readings. The water level in the bottle should mirror any changes displayed in altitude. Keep a close track of the location and always be aware of the closest airports at any point in time. In case the pilot needs to make an unscheduled landing and is disoriented, you can give him his options in a jiffy. Also stay extra alert when the plane is above busy cities such as Frankfurt, London, New York, etc. Chances of mid-air collisions are naturally higher in areas with more air traffic.

The concerns arise when your data and assumptions don't seem to correlate to what the pilot is doing, or if the data seems inaccurate. It happened to me once.

I was seated in a creaky old plane from Kuala Lumpur to Mumbai, closely monitoring the flight data on my video screen. The plane seemed to be ascending, but the altitude readings weren't changing. I did the water bottle test and sure enough, the plane was climbing though this was not reflected on my screen.

I called the stewardess and told her that there was some serious problem with the data. She mumbled something under her breath and swayed away. I waited another ten minutes and then demanded to speak to her supervisor. A man in a jacket came and I told him what the problem was – that the plane was climbing at a rate that was not reflected in the data. Was the captain aware of this life-threatening situation, I asked.

"Let me assure you sir, the captain is not relying on this system to fly the plane," he said, with a hint of sarcasm.

"Are you sure?" I screeched apprehensively.

"I swear on my wife's nasi lemak," he said, pinching his throat.

"Liar, liar, pants on fire," I mumbled under my breath. And I focused on my praying lips all the way to Chhatrapati Shivaji International Airport.

BEYOND THE SAFETY INFORMATION CARD

"If black boxes can survive air-crashes,
why don't they make the whole plane out of that stuff?"
— George Carlin

While no plane has yet collided with the sky, mid-air fender benders with other aircraft do occur. You'd think that two little specs of hurtling metal in the earth's vast atmosphere could manage to avoid each other. But that is not always the case.

If you are seated at the window, it is your moral duty to help avoid a mid-air collision. So keep your nose glued to the window, eyes scanning the horizon and watch for any approaching aircraft. If you see a plane dangerously close, yell, *"Watch Out!"*

"Captain! Look out! We have a giraffe to the left!!"

If you do happen to find yourself in a situation where your plane is losing the battle against gravity, adopt the classic brace position that airlines propound. Place your feet flat on the ground, head bent low on the seat in front of you and hands above your head or under your thighs.

Ignore the conspiracy theories that the brace position is only intended to preserve the teeth of victims so that dental records can be used to identify bodies. Or that it is actually more likely to kill a person than save him, since it's cheaper for airlines to pay compensation for wrongful death rather than continuous injury. Ignore that bunk – no one can argue with the fact that when you are plummeting to earth from 38,000 feet, bending low and bracing for impact will certainly help you survive.

LEARNING FROM THE AUTO INDUSTRY

If a $10,000 car can be fitted with six air bags, a $100 million plane can conceivably afford to have 60,000. All I am asking for is a measly 200 – one air bag for each seat.

It is such a comfort though, isn't it, to see a Rolls-Royce engine on the wing? You just believe that nothing will go wrong.

I wish my car had one of them babies as well.

DEALING WITH RASCALS

The standard protocol if a plane gets hijacked is for the crew to hand over a memo to the hijacker that generally starts, 'To whomsoever it may concern'. It goes on to mention that the crew will cooperate with the hijacker, that the safety of the airplane is secondary to that of passengers, and so on.

Since the industry's brilliant first line of defense is a stunning memo, it needs to be given in triplicate: the hijacker keeping one copy for his records and returning two signed and acknowledged copies. After verifying his signature against any standard government-issued ID, the crew sends one copy to the cockpit and one for archival to head office.

The good news is that as part of the industry's ongoing Go Green initiative, all this unnecessary paperwork is moving online and the memo will henceforth be emailed to the hijacker with a 'cc' to the captain. Passengers will also have an opportunity to 'Like' and 'Comment' via their Facebook accounts.

The bad news is that I am only making *some* of this up.

The second line of defense, if the darn memo doesn't move the hijacker to a tearful surrender, is an axe in the cockpit. I swear I am not kidding you. Listen up you evil hijacker, our pilots *Braveheart Mel* and *Gladiator Crowe* are now going to demonstrate their proficiency with medieval weapons.

"My name is Captimus Aximus Hijaximus.
And I will have my vengeance, in this flight or the next."

If you own a private jet, you should exercise caution if you are parking it overnight in an airport, especially in dark, secluded spots. Criminals are usually lurking in the shadows waiting to break in and fly away.

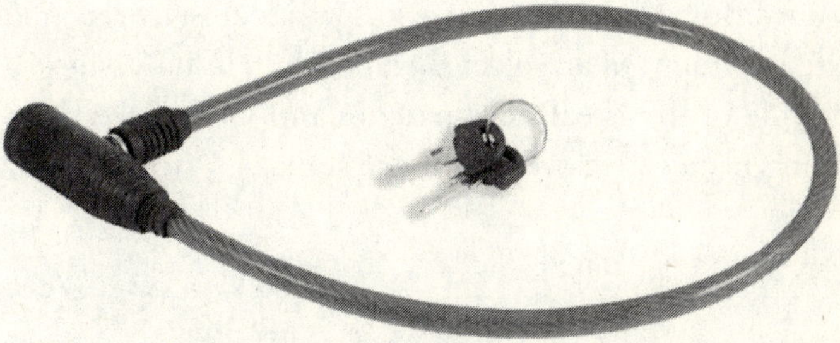

This week's bargain! Flexible steel cable airplane locks. Available in red, blue and black.

I strongly recommend that unless it was anyway headed to the Salvation Army, do not give your jacket to the attendant to stow in the coat closet. You may not be aware of this, but there is a deadly global jacket mafia that operates in the skies. They possess their own planes and fly around looking for aircraft that have the cabin lights dimmed. When they spot a likely prey, they pull alongside and in a daring mid-air maneuver attach cables and zip-line across to board the target.

Once inside, they quickly make their way to the coat closet and pull out just one jacket and beat a hasty retreat. For them, it has been a completely random selection; for you, it's an absolute certainty that the jacket was yours. And the attendant can make all the *"If anyone has mistakenly taken a navy blue jacket, please identify yourself"* announcements that she goddamn wants. But your jacket, as we know, has already reached the basement of an unmarked building in Italy where a couple of thugs with eye patches and tattoos are high-fiving each other over Sambuca shots.

"Let's swipe one of those plastic headphones as well, while we are at it."

YOUR SAFETY IS OUR PRIMARY CONCERN

The life vest is like the Loch Ness Monster: people say it exists, but no one is really sure. Check if it is really where the attendant is saying it is – under the seat or in a compartment above you. Test it for fit and snugness and pull the cord to make sure that it inflates. Ignore the strange looks from your neighbor. That nitwit can sink like a stone while you breast-stroke away from a sinking plane in a secure and operational life vest.

*"Directions to the Caribbean?
Paddle straight ahead 4,000 miles, then hang a sharp right and go 1,500 miles till you reach a big wave..."*

In the event of crashing on water, remember also that the seat cushions can be used as flotation devices. That's really useful – crashing into the middle of the Atlantic and then paddling away to North America on a freaking airline cushion.

I would please like to review some statistics on what percentage of passengers who ever slid down the emergency chute, removed their shoes before doing so.

"The plane is on fire, honey! The plane is going to blow up!"

"Stop shrieking, woman, and take off your stilettos first."

When dipped in water, the emergency chute apparently transforms into a life raft. And the stewardess into Megan Fox.

I really don't understand why people don't do this, but for about $2,000, on a plethora of Internet sites, one can buy item six, an operational parachute – a self-contained little canvas package that can be strapped comfortably to one's body. Imagine the peace of mind! While the flight attendants are droning on and on about seat belts, life vests and other utterly useless safety devices, just turn to your neighbor and pat your parachute with a grin. And bask in the look of envy you will receive.

"You mean you are out of Pepsi? I can't take this any more. Your airline sucks. That's it, I'm gone!"

In the event of sudden loss of cabin pressure, oxygen masks will descend from the roof like Tom Cruise in *Mission Impossible.* The situation is nothing like the safety videos where passengers lean over with a smile, pull the mask toward them and adjust it around their nose, as if all of this is just a minor irritant on a perfectly routine flight. If this were to actually happen while you are mid-air, stop screaming four-letter words, pull the mask over your face and breathe like there is no tomorrow. If you are traveling with children, depending on how much you love them, secure your mask before assisting with theirs. If you are traveling with your wife, be courteous and first offer her mask to your neighbor.

CLIMATE CONTROL

If you happen to be on a propeller plane, you can adjust the cabin temperature through a switch on your seat that regulates those large fans on the wings. Don't shut off the fans completely though as people will start sweating, for reasons other than just heat.

If people are sweating, don't open the emergency exit door or roll down the window to let in some breeze. That is not a good idea.

On the other hand, if you feel cold you can ask the attendant for what is popularly known as a blanket. They are usually always *out of blankets,* but in case they are *in of blankets,* he or she will get you one. It's a piece of sheer cloth, slightly complicated to operate and does little to keep you warm. However, it has an innovative rectangular design and you can knot a few of them together to make a lovely Arabian tent across your row of seats.

Or you could use it as an emergency parachute; just grip the ends tightly and gently float away to earth from 38,000 feet. I haven't tested this, but as a kid I never faced any malfunctions when I tied stones to dad's handkerchiefs and flung them off the eighth floor... apart from the one time that I cracked Mehta uncle's windshield.

TECHNICAL SNAGS

'Technical Snag' has been used liberally by airlines as a catchall phrase to explain anything and everything that goes wrong. The flight has been delayed, the aircraft is being changed, the plane is returning to the airport – all due to a 'technical snag'.

About 90% of technical snags revolve around punctured tires and ignition problems. As per my packing list, always carry a stepney, jack and jumper cables in your hand baggage and you can help the airline resolve them on the spot.

Be careful if the technical snag is in the latter 10%. Absolutely refuse to get onto a plane that had a delay due to a technical snag, which has now been 'fixed'. What if the mechanic did a shoddy job – will you find out, to your dismay, while you are mid-air? Ask the pilot to first take the plane for a spin and do a few loops and turns in the air. Once it has been clearly established that the snag has indeed been fixed, you can board the plane. *Capisce?*

If you are seeking slightly more esoteric ways to deal with technical snags, you can learn from Nepal Airways. Their preferred method for fixing mechanical problems is to sacrifice goats on the runway in front of the grounded plane. This is done to appease *Akash Bhairab,* who is considered by Hindus to be the god who protects those in the sky. The airline proudly noted that after a particular ceremony in September 2007, the concerned plane successfully managed to fly to Hong Kong without crashing.

GO-AROUNDS

The only thing that is worse than a go-around is a crash landing. A go-around occurs when the plane is close to ground, with the landing gear deployed and 400 ears perk up to hear rubber smooching asphalt. Suddenly there is a powerful roar and inches from landing, the plane takes off and climbs rapidly. The captain had obviously encountered something so incredibly dangerous that landing had to be aborted. Like a deer in his path. Or forty knot crosswinds. Or the realization that he had mistaken the Western Express highway for a darned runway.

Go-arounds are essentially super-sized panic and heart attacks rolled into one. And all you can do is hope that at some point, whether it's planes or planets, they will always align in the way you would wish. But until then, it's *Power Up, Nose Up, Gear Up, Flaps Up, Shut Up, Go-Around.*

"Stop hounding me. Go-around. Go as in 'scoot'. Around as in 'any which way'. Go-around!"

LOOS, BOOZE AND THE FOOD YOU CHOOSE

"When you think about flying, it's nuts really. Here you are at about 40,000 feet, screaming along at 700 miles an hour, and you're sitting there drinking Diet Pepsi and eating peanuts. It just doesn't make any sense."

— David Letterman

It's time to focus on some of the other activities that occupy much of people's time on flights. Food ingestion, digestion and so on.

LOOS

Do not ask the flight attendants for the men's room. There are none. The universal sign for restrooms, to be used by both men and women, on most airlines is:

Unless you are flying within stunning eastern Europe, in which case it is:

It is generally advocated that one should not flush while still sitting on the throne. Finish your business, get up and only then hit the flush button. Airplanes are equipped with state-of-the-art vacuum flushes that use brute suction power to pull out all the crap. If you operate the flush while still on the pot, there is a reasonable chance that your intestines may get ripped out through your ass.

While there are signs in most bathrooms requesting that you wipe down the basin as a favor to the next passenger, it's impossible to do so without having something go terribly wrong. The faucet leaks, the napkin tears or the sink stopper gets stuck. To hell with the next passenger – just leave the basin, wet as it is.

The Mile High Club is an urban myth. Airplane lavatories can barely contain two butt cheeks, let alone two people copulating.

There is a sign above the basin that says the water is not for drinking. Okay, thanks for letting me know. Because I usually love to drink water from bathrooms.

Has anyone in the world paid the $2,000 federal fine for tampering with the smoke detector in the airplane lavatory?

Anyone? Anyone at all? Madame Tussauds called, wanting to install a statue of you.

What lopsided mechanical engineering principles have been used to design the faucets in the airplane lavatories? There is one red rectangular knob for hot water and a blue one for cold water. So far, so good. Water flows as you hold the knob down and stops immediately as you let it go. And it is therefore not humanly possible to wash both your hands together; to keep the blasted water running, one hand needs to press the knob at all times.

Some people manage to operate the faucet with their elbows but I prefer to use my chin. Pull out the eight item on my packing list – a little cushioning pad, place it over your chin, lean over and use your chin to press the knob down. Yes, I appreciate that your neck muscles will strain painfully but give me a break, we are just quickly washing hands here, not having a bubble bath.

The faucets at the airport restrooms are no better. They are generally motion activated – you need to rub your hands together in front of a sensor and the water hopefully starts to run. *Yeah right.* Most goddamn annoying thing in the world – you keep waving your hands in front of the inanimate tap but all you hear are empty little clicks. After minutes of frustrating inactivity, you start moving from basin to basin, flapping your palms like a raving lunatic, hoping that at least one of them will start dispensing water.

It is at times like these that I really wish I were a sultan.

I would just clap my hands and someone would appear to wash the royal bum.

Dum-maro-dum... mit jaye gum... bolo subah sham... Hare Krishna Hare Ram (English Translation: Puff, have a puff. Wipe out your sorrows. Chant morning-evening. Hare Krishna Hare Ram).

IN-FLIGHT MEALS

I have never understood the song and dance around meals; is it really necessary, serving a sandwich and juice, on a 90-minute flight? But then I figured that it's just another ploy by the airline industry to keep the attendants occupied.

If you're on the aisle seat, be the first in your row to take a meal tray and the last to return it. The idea is that at any point, if there is an attendant handling food trays around you, your tray table should be down. You can encounter turbulence, attendants can be clumsy, co-passengers can be tipsy and you want to avoid coffee stains or ketchup down the front of your pants. So your tray table can provide a useful layer of protection when you hear *"Ooops"*, followed by a thud, followed by *"Oh sir, I am so sorry!"*

"It's still rare. I wanted it well done. I want to see the chef. NOW!"

Before the actual meal service starts, attendants sway around delivering the 'special meals' to passengers who had pre-requested them. There is a good chance that you will be saddled with one, just because your luck is so awesome. She will come and slam a tray on your table: *"Your special meal, sir."* As you shake your head vigorously, indicating that you didn't ask for one, she shoves a dot-matrixed printout in front of your face, *"Seat 14C, See. Hindu Meal. See. 14C. See. Aren't you 14C?"* You look at your boarding card, desperately hoping that the seat number printed on it has magically changed since you last saw it 30 minutes ago. But it hasn't.

"But I don't want this Hindu meal, Ma'am. I don't even know what a Hindu meal is. Is it what I eat every day at home, like a billion other Indians? Can I please try the Thai green curry rice? Pleaaaaaaaase..."

But by now she is at 18A, slamming a bowl of chopped watermelon and papaya on the table of a wannabe investment banker.

Sometimes it can take really long for the meal service to get started. If you are extremely hungry and impatient, just raise your hand and ask the attendant if she can at least serve you some appetizers. If she's not very busy, she will be happy to go to the galley and fry you a batch of fresh, hot *bhajiyas.*

Airline food is generally very bland. But thankfully you have followed my advice and carried your masala dabba (spice box) on board. A basic masala dabba contains *haldi* (turmeric), *jeera* (cumin), *lal mirch* (red chilli), *hing* (asafetida), *dhania* (coriander) and *garam masala* (hot ground mixture). Mix all of these together in a spoonful of oil to make a nice *tadka* (a garnish of Indian spices) and sprinkle over your food. Yummy.

A *tadka,* however perfect you make it, may not go well with certain cuisines, like Italian or Chinese for example. So make sure you also carry a bottle of Tabasco – it goes well with everything, except maybe chocolate cake and strawberry ice cream. It also comes in cute and convenient two and five ounce miniature bottles that pass through security without a hitch. Airline food will never be the same again.

If you are an atheist, jump to the next section. If you are still reading this, I assume that you believe in God. At 38,000 feet, believing in God has real implications. If you are a good man, you are closer to His hand of blessing. But if you are evil, He can just hurl a thunderbolt your way, as your plane passes the cloud He is sitting on.

I personally try to not provoke God when I am flying, so while in the air, I do all the things that I think He would appreciate. I do not pull out my laptop if it's a

Sunday. And I do not covet my neighbor's wife, male or female servants, or oxen (if they happen to be on the same flight). And I eat only vegetarian meals in the sky – just in case He is a PETA supporter. I can live with consuming only fiber on a 90-minute flight – why take a chance with Him?

"Tsk-Tsk. You should have stayed away from the lamb kebabs, my child..."

Speaking of fiber, what is it that suddenly makes everyone want to drink tomato juice on flights? Do you ever drink that insipid liquid at home?

An echo is a reflection of sound that reaches the

listener some time after the direct sound is made. Some examples are the echoes produced at the bottom of a well, in a valley or in an empty room.

You can also experience the phenomenon of echoes during meal service. If you are still hungry after eating that bird-sized portion, ask the attendant for another meal. And then sit back and listen to the echoes.

You to attendant: *"I want another meal."*

Attendant to you: *"You want another meal?"*

Attendant to colleague: *"He wants another meal!"*

Colleague to attendant: *"He wants another meal?"*

Attendant and colleague to Chief Attendant: *"He wants another meal!"*

Chief Attendant to all passengers: *"He wants another meal!!"*

All passengers to each other: "*He wants another meal??*"

"Everyone together as the wave comes around – HE WANTS ANOTHER MEAL!!!"

If your name isn't Daniel Craig, how do you differentiate yourself from the other 199 passengers on board? The answer is 'clean meal tray'. Post meal service is probably the worst part of a flight attendant's job. Who can enjoy going from seat to seat, collecting messy trays of food, with oily napkins and crumb-laden cutlery hanging from the sides?

Now imagine her reaction when she comes around to your seat, and waiting for her is a nice clean tray, used cutlery packed back neatly into the plastic pouch, napkin nicely folded, empty water bottle laid horizontally across, and everything looking spic and span. She looks at the tray in admiration, looks at you with affection, picks it up and whispers, *"Thank you, sir,"* as she kneels to stow it into her food trolley.

And for the rest of the flight, she beams broadly at you every time she sways by.

On the other hand, nothing agitates an attendant more than you walking up behind him, as he is working the food trolley, and saying, *"Excuse me, can I get through?"* He turns around, rolls his eyes all the way back into the sockets and exercises an extraordinary amount of restraint to stop himself from picking up that plastic knife and stabbing you straight through the heart. If you have people at home who would be glad to welcome you back, quietly go back to your seat.

BOOZE

At some point in time, in a nondescript conference room, in the office of some startup airline that has since failed, some bright-eyed summer intern must have raised his or her hand and innocently suggested, *"Why don't we serve liquor on flights?"* And that person deserves a statue in every airport terminal across the world, as a mark of respect and appreciation. Because that is like the most awesome idea that the airline industry has come up with, since the days of Kitty Hawk.

There was a time when the boring dads would collect postage stamps. And the cool dads would collect miniature liquor bottles handed out by stewardesses.

There was a time when the whisky they served me on flights was older than I was.

There was a time when you could smoke on flights. The rear of the plane was reserved for smokers and they would drink like fish and puff like chimneys. The attendants would come by ever so often to sneak in a few swigs and drags as well. One would pass time by demonstrating cool Zippo lighter tricks to co-passengers and it was all one big, happy Woodstock festival between rows 35 to 42.

Until someone realized that playing with fire, sitting atop 50,000 gallons of jet fuel at 38,000 feet, was not such a bright idea.

"And now, dear passengers, put your hands together for our next live, in-flight performance. Vasili, the fire-eater!"

Sometimes when I can't decide between white wine and red, I have a pink. I take half a glass of red, half a glass of white, and stir it together. I always get strange looks from the attendant but I can't really blame her. We are more of a whisky-drinking nation and she probably doesn't encounter too many Indians like me, who truly appreciate fine wines.

If I ever see an attendant who is even a wee bit enthusiastic about pushing that duty-free goods trolley down the aisle, I promise I will buy a liter of hooch.

If you don't have at least one "I was so drunk when I reached the airport" anecdote to share, you really haven't lived your life. So go ahead and do it – party all night, get wasted, go straight to the airport, somehow board the flight and then drink some more.

The world awaits your story.

In the good old days when I did not need hair color (it's only on my sideburns, please note), I had a lot of "I was so drunk" stories. But there is nothing interesting to relate about them – puking in the check-in line or passing out in the aisle of a plane – no big deal, it used to happen all the time.

However, I do remember an interesting coincidence that occurred when I was flying from Madrid to New York, after an especially raucous New Year celebration. And it has nothing to do with being drunk.

I was sitting stone cold hammered at the terminal in Barajas airport, barely able to keep my eyes open.

I was supposed to be on a plane to New York's JFK airport and Spain, in the late '90s, was not really the most popular destination for Indian tourists. And as I am sitting there, swaying on my seat, I keep hearing, alternately in English and Spanish, *"American Airlines paging Rishi Piparaiya."* Or *"Rishi Piparaiya, you need to board your flight to New York immediately."*

And I thought, *"Wow! Here I am, all the way in Madrid, and there is another passenger, also named Rishi Piparaiya, who is also flying to New York. What are the odds of that happening!"*

And I continued sitting there, plastered, listening to those increasingly frantic announcements. And I hope that the other Rishi Piparaiya made his flight.

WHAT THE HECK, CAPTAIN!

"The warm Hawaiian sun was blaring in, as we went eastbound. I just closed my eyes for a minute, enjoying the sunshine and dozed off."

— From the NTSB interview with a captain, who along with the first officer, fell asleep, heading out over the ocean during a flight from Honolulu to Hilo. They awoke in time to fly back to land.

When you board a plane, you have put your life in the hands of a complete stranger, who is usually too young to handle a car, let alone a 400-ton aircraft. There are a host of items that one needs to be cognizant of when it comes to pilots and you should never hesitate to jump up from your seat and yell at the top of your lungs, *"What the heck, Captain!"*

If the captain boards the plane and heads straight for the cockpit, yank him out by the collar. Shouldn't he be taking a walk around the plane, inspecting the body for cracks, tapping the engines, kicking the tires to check on air pressure and so on? Isn't that what people do when they are going on a road trip, so why is flying any different?

Body tackle the attendant if she is taking meal trays to the cockpit during the flight. The damn sandwiches can wait and can we get our priorities right, please? Hello, we have a plane to fly.

Ever noticed how often captains leave the cockpit to go to the bathroom? On every flight I am on, either one or both pilots take turns to go take a piddle. I can understand the need for a quick wee-wee on, let's say, a transatlantic flight. But can't you hold it in for the duration of a quick Mumbai-Delhi hop?

Fling a bottle in his direction, if you see the captain exiting the cockpit to use the loo. He can use it to pee in, while staying put at his seat instead. No one leaves the cockpit on your watch.

"When I grow up, I want to become a pilot."

Captains who leave the cockpit to make conversation with friends in business class should be hung from the wings at 38,000 feet. Pilots who venture all the way to economy, to say hello to passengers, could be given a hug, but then still need to be shot. In this networked world of mobile phones, BlackBerry, Whatsapp, Facebook, Twitter, and whatnot, do they really need to step out, mid-flight that too, to make conversation?

Pilots sometimes cover the windshield with newspapers to block out sunlight. Are you kidding me? Tint the windows, wear sunglasses, use your palm on your forehead as a visor, but leave your line of sight clear, for God's sake. Peek into the cockpit and throw a fit if you see this happening.

OTHER ASPECTS OF CAPTAINCY

If you have any technical questions about the airplane, feel free to ask the captain. If you are not satisfied with his answer, ask for the instructions manual that came along with the airplane. It will be a little booklet wrapped in plastic and you should be able to find it, dust-coated but unopened, at the bottom of the cardboard carton that the plane was shipped in. Along with the extra wires and the AAA remote control batteries.

How is it that pilots travel with such tiny suitcases and yet their clothes are always freshly ironed, crisply starched and as white as a pilot's clothes? What's their secret? Does a *dhobi* tag along on the jump seat?

*"I really don't enjoy the stints abroad.
You just don't get these facilities on the Hudson or Thames."*

And why do all pilots, whether men or women, wear ties? Do they all go to the opera upon landing?

An experienced pilot earns well over $100,000 and flies about 800 hours a year. That's $125 an hour for essentially playing *Flight Simulator*. He has no monthly goals, no boss and all his colleagues are hot. The job calls for some travel yes, but stay is at luxury hotels, meals are included and life is one long MTV Grind party.

I have a 9 to 5 job – 9 am to 5 am. I work 365 days a year, looking forward to leap years when I get a day off. I have stiff monthly sales targets and a boss who roams around in a patent leather jacket and brandishes a whip. I get paid peanuts, three bags reaching home every month, and I supplement my meager income by writing paperbacks during bathroom breaks for 10% author royalty. I am, what is known in aviation parlance, a 'low-cost career'.

But I have never gone on strike a single day in the 15 years of my working life.

In some cultures, it is customary to deliver a vote of thanks to the pilot at the end of a flight. You should take the lead on this if other passengers are bashful. Just identify yourself to the flight attendant as the person who will be proposing the vote and settle in at his or her landing station. As the plane lands and taxis to the gate, announce to the cabin, *"Dear all, please join me in thanking our captain for getting us here safe and sound etc..."* Sprinkle some humor by poking fun at any mistakes he made during the flight or describing any scary moments that you all went through. That always draws some laughs.

Grace is a virtue that is rapidly heading towards extinction, but once in a while you see the captain and the co-pilot standing smartly at attention outside the cockpit, smiling at passengers as they disembark. This gesture I think is the epitome of good customer service, and while I don't know what the protocol is, I pull out a few tenners from my wallet and whisper a "Good landing, my men" while patting them on the shoulders in appreciation. I don't really want to draw much attention to my kindheartedness, so I simply slip the bills into their palms or, better yet, into their shirt pocket with a finger on my lips. Shush. No one needs to know.

ANNOUNCEMENTS FROM THE COCKPIT

I think it is an unsaid job requirement – pilots need to have bad diction. Listen to the captain's announcements on the public address system very carefully. Look out for pronunciation, quality of English, pace of speech and so on. It's not his interaction with the cabin that concerns you, but his communication with Air Traffic Control that will determine whether you make it to ground in peace, or pieces.

So do not be shy to slip him a note with useful tips – *"Dear Captain, thank you for your report on the weather enroute. In general, can I ask you to speak a bit slower and enunciate your vowels a little more? Your well-wisher in seat 14C."*

If you are flying internationally, the captain will first make his announcements in the local language and then repeat it in some alleged dialect of English. Pay close attention to the local language version – you obviously can't understand what he is saying but observe the reactions of the passengers. If they have not started shrieking and screaming, it means that all is probably okay with the plane.

That said, here are some announcements that you don't want to hear in any language.

- *"Ladies and Gentlemen, this is your Captain speaking. Am having some ummm... technical difficulties here – does anyone in the cabin know how to help fly a Boeing?"*

- *"Can someone remind me, where are we heading to today?"*

- *"Can the tall gentleman in 28E please be seated? You are blocking my rear view mirror."*

- *"Folks, the autopilot system has hung and I need to Control-Alt-Delete. We will be plummeting approximately 25,000 feet until it reboots – please do fasten your seatbelts."*

- *"Can I have your attention please? Does someone have a map of the Middle East? This darn GPS doesn't seem to be working."*

- *"Aaand we would (hic) like (hic) to thank youuuh forrr flying (hic) our ayerline (slur)."*

ABSOLUTELY TRUE 'WHAT THE HECK' STORIES

Inspired by assorted news articles, here are some 'What the Heck, Captain!' incidents that, unbelievable as they sound, have truly occurred.

"Happy birthday to me, happy birthday to me...."

We've all had one of those wild birthday parties with an overdose of cake, piñatas and of course, alcohol. So did Captain Alexander who celebrated his 55th birthday on a cold evening in December 2008, and reported to fly an Aeroflot flight from Moscow to New York soon after. Settling into his cockpit seat, he proceeded to welcome his passengers with so garbled a message that it generated mass hysteria on the plane.

"His speech was so slurred, it was hard to tell what language he was speaking," said one passenger. When a larger group started protesting the scenario of being flown halfway around the world by a vodka bottle with stripes, they were told to *"stop making trouble"*.

The passengers demanded to see the pilot to verify his sobriety but were told that he was busy in the cockpit, *"with his foot on the brake"*. As the deadlock continued, Alexander finally stumbled out with a red face, bloodshot eyes and posed an incredulous *"Do I look drunk to you?" "Yes!"* the passengers chorused; there being little ambiguity on what a drunk Russian looks like.

A few hours later a new crew boarded and the flight finally took off, at a clean horizontal angle. Aeroflot tried to subsequently extricate itself from this sticky situation using every conceivable excuse in the book, including claiming that the pilot *"may have suffered a stroke"* before making his incoherent pre-flight announcement to passengers.

They ended by saying that they don't really understand what this whole brouhaha is about because anyway, *"It's not such a big deal if the pilot is drunk. Really, all he has to do is press a button and the plane flies itself. The worst that could happen is he'll trip over something in the cockpit."*

Northwest 188 was on a routine flight from San Diego to Minneapolis-St. Paul when the cockpit went strangely silent for over an hour. The plane overshot Minneapolis by 150 miles, merrily chugging along to the panic of ATC officers and other pilots in the vicinity. As the US President prepared to press the red nuclear button, fighter jets were scrambled and lined up, ready to take off and blow the plane out of the sky.

Thankfully, before the world heard *Geronimo* at 38,000 feet, the pilots sheepishly called in with a *"Ah, roger, ah, we got, ah, distracted and we've overflown, ah, Minneapolis. We are overhead Eau Claire and would like to make a one-eighty and do our arrival from Eau Claire."*

What apparently had transpired was that the two dudes had pulled out their personal laptops to understand a new crew flight scheduling system that their company

"This is so much fun. Once again. Miss Mary Mack, Mack, Mack, all dressed in black, black…"

had put in place. They were in such a 'concentrated period of discussion' that they missed all the frenzy around them, realizing their situation only when a flight attendant called to check when exactly it was that they were landing.

The 144 passengers, three flight attendants, two pilots and two laptops landed safely about an hour after the originally scheduled time.

A pilot for Sriwijaya Air in Indonesia landed his plane, a Boeing 737, that too, at the wrong airport. The plane carrying 102 passengers and crew was supposed to land at Padang's Minangkabau International airport. Instead it landed at Tabing Air Force base, 12 kilometers away. A ministry spokesman said that the pilot had been suspended and asked for an explanation. And the officials at Minangkabau airport were also questioned.

Luckily the investigations ended up all clear – the landing apparently was perfectly normal, besides the minor point of it being at the wrong airport.

"What do I do? They all look the same from the air – white paint on grey concrete. It's just trial and error for me."

"Eenie, Meenie, Miney, Mo, catch a tiger by its toe, with which button shall I go, Eenie, Meenie...."

I can imagine cockpits to be fairly complicated, with hundreds of switches and buttons jostling for the captain's attention. You would hope that pilots stand a fair chance at getting it right, unlike the captain of a British Airways flight from London to Hong Kong.

He mistakenly pushed a switch that played a pre-recorded message in a sexy, sultry female voice, just as the plane was over the North Sea. Nothing very ominous, oh, just that this was *"an emergency announcement and that we may shortly need to make an emergency landing on water."*

As the 275 terrified passengers hurriedly changed into their swimming trunks, cabin crew realized the mistake and swayed down the aisles trying to explain it away as the wry British sense of humor. No one was particularly amused, least of all Captain Butterfingers who was shit scared of tapping any other button for the rest of the flight.

British Scareways regretted the 'undue distress'.

What's the first thing you do when you get into the driver's seat of a car? Adjust the mirrors and the seat right? Well, our co-pilot in the next story waited till he was halfway to outer space to do either, with the expected consequences.

A 25-year-old co-pilot on an Air India Express flight from Dubai to Pune decided to adjust his seat while in mid-air. As he did so, he inadvertently pressed the control column forward, which pushed the plane into an uncontrollable dive. And this time the plane dove 7,000 feet. And this too, bang in the middle of meal service, so now you had chicken tikka masala fogging the cabin at a 26-degree angle.

But there was a captain to help stabilize the plane right? No! In a scene that is as familiar as it is disturbing, the captain was, where else, in the loo, on what else, a bathroom break. So 25-year-old Chunnu Munnu, just about legally allowed to have a beer, froze completely. According to the Directorate General of Civil Aviation, who I am assuming is the big cheese of flights in India, he *"probably had no clue how to tackle this kind of emergency."*

Luckily, the captain had a code and managed to zip up his trousers and access the cockpit while his colleague was still playing 'L-O-N-D-O-N London Statue!' in his now comfortably adjusted seat. He leveled the aircraft before it slammed into the ground, an event that would have, in all probability, readjusted all the seats on the plane. And he then calmly announced that the plane *"went through an air pocket, and that is why there was a rapid descent."*

And everyone breathed a sigh of relief and went back to their desserts.

Badly timed leaks are the biggest source of concern to fliers around the world.

The last few days had taken their toll. A long onward flight, a couple of meetings with colleagues, and then, of course, the late nights out on the town. Now he was finally back on a nine-hour flight to Brussels – a lazy destination that he was quite looking forward to unwinding at. I must stay awake, he thought. It will take me days to recover from the jet lag if I sleep on this flight.

She scanned the inbox on her Android tablet – an acquisition from her last trip to the fashionable Rue Neuve. Three days on the road and all that clubbing with colleagues had disrupted her schedule – how she longed for her nightly routine in the comfort of a soft bed, where she could catch up on her mails before she dozed off to sleep.

It was calm, without the slightest trace of turbulence, and the hum of the engines had lulled most of the cabin to sleep. "We must be around Istanbul," she said, looking over at her companion. But he was fast asleep as well. "The poor dear," she murmured, deciding against putting the curls on his forehead back in place, lest she unwittingly wake him up. And freed of the compulsion to make any further polite conversation, she focused on her tablet, reviewing her inbox with her characteristic intensity.

The moonlight skidded off its polished wings as the Jet Airways plane from Mumbai to Brussels glided down through the hospitable Turkish airspace. It was quite the perfect flight. But for the holy, freaking moly fact that he was the pilot and she was the co-pilot and they were supposed to be flying the damn airplane. But he was fast asleep and she was 'busy on her tablet'. And the plane dropped 5,000 feet over Ankara before a freaked-out Air Traffic Control managed to connect with them.

Passengers with deadly contagious diseases shouldn't be allowed to fly. That's reasonable. So I don't know what the big deal was in kicking out a 16-year-old schoolgirl from a Newark to Honolulu flight. After all, she was inflicted with a bout of – drum roll please – coughing.

Yes, that's exactly what happened to Rachel who caught a cold while on a school trip to New York. So she started coughing uncontrollably just before takeoff. The Continental Airlines attendants gave her a glass of water and a doctor on board certified that she was perfectly okay to fly. But Captain Doolittle kicked her and her teacher out anyway and they were left to fend for themselves on the wicked streets of Manhattan.

The good news is that her inconsolable sobbing, as she got booted out, magically cured the coughing.

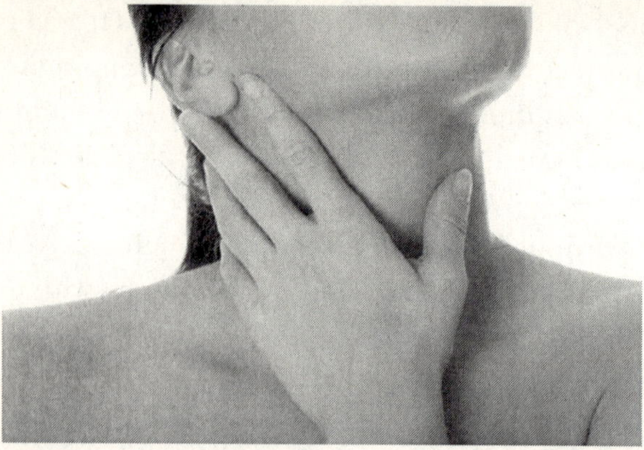

"Gale mein khich-khich, gale mein khich-khich, kya karoon?" (English translation: My throat scratchy-scratchy, my throat scratchy-scratchy, what do I do?)

We can't let just the captains take all the slack, can we? So here are some incredible anecdotes about passengers, flight crews and their remarkable airplane journeys.

You know how babies keep repeating the same thing over and over again. Like five hundred thousand times. Well 19-month-old Baby Garren decided to say *"Bye Bye Plane"* as his Continental Express jet to Atlanta pulled out from the gate at Houston airport. And he kept repeating it as the flight attendant went through her boring safety drill. *Bye Bye Plane. Bye Bye Plane. Bye Bye Plane.*

Now, rather than pulling his chubby cheeks with an *"Ooooh cho chweeet"*, the attendant instead got rather annoyed. And she leaned over and told Garren's mother, *"You need to shut your baby up."* As the surprised mother explained that he would sleep soon, the attendant suggested she give him allergy medication to hasten the process with, *"It's called Baby Benadryl."*

An argument obviously ensued and the attendant complained to the captain that she had been threatened. So the captain promptly turned the plane and headed back to the gate and threw Mother Garren and Baby Garren out.

"Mirror, Mirror on the wall, who's the meanest of them all?"

This attendant is a star. A rockstar. A legend.

A JetBlue flight had landed at New York's JFK airport and was moving toward the gate. A passenger got up to get something from the overhead bin while the seat belt signs were still on. So Steven, the attendant, asked her to sit down. A little argument ensued and as the passenger closed the bin, she bumped Steven on the head. Steven asked for an apology and the passenger, in true Big Apple lingo, told him to *F@#* off.* And that was the end of a 20-year-career in the most stylish manner possible.

Stevie got onto the PA system and launched into an expletive-laden tirade at all passengers as a group. Ending it with *"I've had it. That's it."* And he activated the emergency chute, picked two beers from the trolley and popped one open, chucked his carry on bags down, slid down the chute, jumped off a moving plane, ran across the tarmac to the parking lot, and drove home.

Wow! And I get nervous about taking a bathroom break during a conference call with my boss.

When you've spent each day lamenting about how beautifully wondrous life might have been if you were just a few inches taller, you cannot help but snicker at this next one.

A passenger, three inches shy of seven feet, was kicked out of a Horizon Air flight from Portland to Ontario for being too tall. In his defense, he did make all attempts to get an exit row seat when he purchased his ticket.

He tried again for an exit seat at check-in but was told that his *"long limbs are now the flight attendant's problem."*

And obviously, the flight attendant didn't like this problem because she kept tripping on Daddy Long Legs, who was stretched out as far as a few rows ahead. So she asked him to keep his legs within the confines of his seat. Which try as he might, given the limitations of human anatomy and seat physics, the poor chap could not comply with. The airline, presumably, gave him an option to go for a double amputation at the knees, but the selfish passenger declined.

So off the flight he was asked to go.

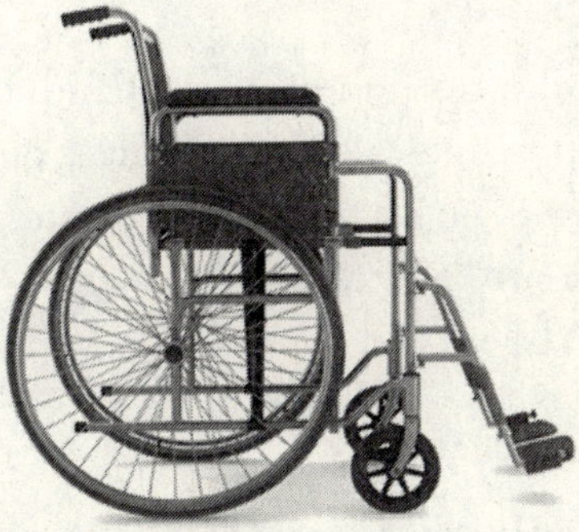

"Sir, we don't see what the problem is.
It's a quick procedure covered by medical insurance.
And we will also throw in one of these, gratis!"

There are so many air rage incidents that I could write my entire next book about them (publishers anyway tell me that book trilogies are the in-thing). But here are a few examples that are representative of everything that a passenger can do wrong, due to mental instability or alcohol or both.

A man on a Mumbai-Delhi Indigo flight suddenly turned violent and started shouting. When asked to take his seat, he slapped the attendant. He then tried to run into the cockpit and scuffled with all male passengers enroute. A trolley blocked his way so he started waving his mobile phone as if it were a detonator, trying to make a call, and making the gracious offer to all, *"Do you want to go down with me?"*

He was finally restrained with handkerchiefs and scarves but in a final attempt to hit a perfect ten on the bizarro scale, he bit his mobile phone. Which again sent everyone into a tizzy.

James, a property developer was thrilled to be on a Thai Airways flight from Bangkok to London Heathrow. So he quickly took his blood alcohol level from zero to 5.5 times the legal driving limit. And then went on a crazy rampage when he was denied any more booze.

He ran to the bathrooms and emptied all the bins on

the floors, tried to open the aircraft door, headbutted, punched and kicked stewards and tore off his own shirt. And then in a sentimental enactment of 'Love thy neighbor as thyself', he sat on a passenger in the row behind him and spat continually on his face. As in, straddled him and went *Thoo, Thoo, Thoo, Thoo. Swirl, Gargle, Thoooooo.*

Finally out of saliva, he passed out, was restrained, and claimed to have no recollection of the incident when he came to his senses. And when he was arrested upon landing, he tried to get away with a comment that should be familiar to all parents: *"But I've apologized!"*

Three drunken male attendants on a Russian Aviaenergo flight refused to serve wine to the girlfriend of a passenger, possibly to hoard the bottles for themselves. So the passenger put on his 'Chivalry isn't dead' bandana and served up a drink for his Juliet. The three attendants beat him up – they thrashed him so hard that he was left with bruises and a black eye. Having now tasted the sheer joy of hand-to-hand combat at 38,000 feet, they slammed another passenger into the doorway. And started flinging food trays all around the cabin.

A spokesperson for Aeroflop, I mean Aeroflot, which uses the carrier for some domestic routes, explained this new benchmark of customer centricity with a *"You understand how coordination worsens when someone isn't sober."*

Umm... yes... if you say so, Ivana.

Conduct that has so far been restricted to football stadiums in the United Kingdom is now spreading to flights cruising at 38,000 feet.

Seventeen people on a Glasgow to Amsterdam KLM flight were arrested for starting a mid-air riot. They started their drinking binge at Glasgow airport and continued it mid-air. I guess they didn't like the inflight Kenny G piped music, so they initiated their repertoire of highly offensive songs. Oh, and did I mention, they were on their way to attend a concert by a band ironically named, Swedish House Mafia.

Bad singing combined with some good alcohol soon progressed to threatening cabin crew and groping flight attendants. And culminated in a mini riot which ended only upon landing at Schiphol airport.

Thankfully, there were no police vehicles on the flight for them to overturn and burn.

"Thanks sweetheart. Can you get us some Molotov Cocktails next time you come around?"

After a grueling trip through the wilderness of Alaska, adventurous Jeff was heading back home to Portland, Oregon. "I need some water," he murmured as waited to board his JetBlue flight at Anchorage airport, "You never know if these low-cost airline weasels will ensure adequate hydration on board," thirsty Jeff thought as he leaned over, for what was a good five minutes, at the water fountain at the gate. Boarding was announced and tired Jeff, exhausted after weeks of tracking polar bears, caribous and Sarah Palin, fell off to sleep almost instantaneously on his middle seat. Shortly after, the plane took off and started its 3-hour journey southwest.

Now you know the impact that cold air conditioning can have on a full bladder. Half an hour into the flight, sleepy Jeff woke up and looked around – his co-passengers were fast asleep and considerate Jeff didn't want to disturb them. So he stood up, placed his wee-wee between the gap of the two seats in front of him, and then as the saying goes, started to piss like a Russian racehorse at the Kentucky derby. Warm, sticky urine flowed down the arm-rests of the seats in front of carefree Jeff – adding a new dimension of intrigue to the elbow chess matches that were presumably going on. And if that wasn't enough, the plane suddenly lurched and unsteady Jeff fell, pants around his ankles, back onto his seat. And then, like a musical fountain at the Bellagio, his ding-a-ling now started spraying all the people around him. By the time they figured that it was not a leaky cabin roof but gracious Jeff who was responsible for this unexpected condensation, he was once again fast asleep.

Portland cops arrested well-relieved Jeff upon landing for "offensive littering". Dirty Jeff. Bad Jeff.

Hollywood hothead Alec Baldwin was thrown off an American Airlines flight for playing games on his mobile phone while the plane was moving. He apparently took great offence at being asked to stop his 'Words with Friends' session and he flung his papers on the ground and stormed into the loo. Once there he proceeded to bang away at the walls and then returned, swearing at the crew, *"If you want to kick me off, kick me off."*

Well, they took him up on the offer and kicked him off at Los Angeles airport. Luckily there was a Hamleys toy store at the terminal, so he could buy himself a Scrabble board and keep busy.

It's not fair to just single out Alec who I think, in addition to being a grammar whiz, is an outstanding actor (have you seen his performance in *Glengarry Glen Ross?*). So I should mention actor Gerard Depardieu who urinated in the aisle of an Air France airplane. Supermodel Naomi Campbell who threatened, abused, spat on and assaulted crew and officers on a British Airways flight. Rapper Snoop Dogg (since evolved to Snoop Lion) and his entourage who caused a riot at Heathrow, fighting with police officers and smashing a duty-free shop. Mexican singing sensation Paulina Rubio who allegedly punched, slapped and pelted objects at her manager for having the audacity to make her fly economy on a Miami to Mexico flight. Iceland's musical superstar Björk who beat up a photographer for welcoming her to Thailand and then did an action replay at Auckland airport. And actor Ralph Fiennes who set off a million fantasies by making love to a stewardess on an airplane, only to dissociate himself from the entire episode as the damsel lost her job.

The exciting lives that celebrities lead, I tell ya!

AWESOME CO-PASSENGER CONVERSATIONS

Tia: So, he says, "Squeeze your breasts together,"
and I say, "I thought this was an ad for shoes…"
Jerry: Oh my…
— Flight conversation between Jerry and Tia,
a model seated next to him, in the sitcom *Seinfeld.*

By default, you will be sitting next to someone who goes by the single moniker, Shah. *"Call me Shah."* Shah is an unfit bloke whose family comprises Mrs. Shah and three Shah children, Shah, Shah and Shah. Shah is a partner with his brother Shah, at Shah Brothers, an import-export business that is not seeing much traction on either inbound or outbound trades. Shah's cup of woes overfloweth swifter than the Niagara in fast forward. Shah's attempts at opening any conversation should be met by deafening sounds of silence.

Every once in a while you will encounter the big mouth flier. A person who secretly takes pride in the amount he or she flies, while portraying it as a worse ordeal than washing dress shirts in a bidet.

"Last week I was in Chandigarh for the day, took the night flight to Chennai, meetings all day in Chennai, then to Bangalore for a dinner event. Came home to Mumbai on Sunday and today I'm back on this flight to Delhi. Flying for a conference to Singapore day after, and not really sure when I get back to Mumbai again."

I just stare at these people blankly. What's the big deal? Science and technology did all the work; it's not like you were flapping your arms all the way. And if it is indeed such a monumental achievement, why don't you write a book about it? (Note to typesetter: insert eyelashes smiley)

If you are on the next rung of the 'how screwed can my luck be' ladder, you will be seated next to a parent with an infant. Suddenly, crashing doesn't sound like such a bad option now. I don't know why infants need to fly in the first place; it's not like they are going to go, *"Look Ma, the beautiful Eiffel Tower. Thanks for getting me to Paris, Ma."* It probably looks like just another pacifier to them, only bigger and in iron lattice. Leave the kids at home till they reach puberty, is my considered opinion.

If parents still insist on flying with infants, they should strictly be denied in-flight meals. Because they encroach upon your stowaway table before you can say 'meal service'. Their food tray takes center-stage on their table, while all the paraphernalia that comes attached with a baby, is deposited on yours. So suddenly you have diapers, formula bottles and rattles doing the tango with your cutlery, as mom chows down baguettes with one hand and bounces her pamperspooper with the other.

The only solution is to sneak in a few swigs of alcohol into the baby bottle when no one is looking. A little bit of giggle juice in their system and babies will sleep through the flight like, well, babies. Brandy works best, whisky or rum is almost as effective, but do avoid tequila

"Is that right, Uncle? Irish cream is just sweet milk? Sure, pour me a large on the rocks."

shots. It is particularly difficult to get them to lick the salt and suck on a lemon wedge, and that too without Mommy noticing.

But if you are in luck, you may instead be seated next to one of three categories of co-passengers:

- ↗ Off-duty pilots
- ↗ Business tycoons or corporate executives
- ↗ Single and attractive co-passengers

In this section of the book, we shall explore strategies for making your mark and getting the most out of conversations, with each of these groups.

OFF-DUTY PILOTS

It is indeed a pleasure to sit next to off-duty pilots. They are usually in uniform, heading back home for a few days of rest and are in a nice relaxed mood. Off-duty pilots are always polite and treat you like a guest in their home.

The benefits of sitting next to them are immense. They are happy to chat and answer any questions that you may throw at them. I make the most of the opportunity every time I find a pilot seated next to me. It's a rapid quick-fire game of 20 questions and every time I walk off the plane a lot more informed than I used to be. How far can wings flex in turbulence? Which are the various kinds of clouds and which ones should be avoided? How is de-icing done and why? Does lightning impact planes? And so on.

Most importantly, you have Plan B seated right next to you. If anything goes wrong, you have a qualified, competent, licensed flight professional an elbow poke away from you. It's like running a full marathon with a doctor by your side. Or playing Monopoly with an unlimited stack of 'Get Out of Jail Free' cards. Or taking an open book exam. You will hopefully not need it, but if you do, the best possible support is right there.

This is the only time that I make an exception to the 'sit on the aisle seat' rule. If there is an off-duty pilot seated next to me, I insist that he or she take the aisle. I don't want them to have to clamber over me to dash to the cockpit if their services are urgently required. A quick exit is very important and I always give them the rationale for the same.

Actually, and it's always appreciated by all, I prefer to get the pilot, co-pilot and off-duty pilot together for a quick pre-takeoff briefing so we can determine who will do what, in case of an emergency. It is very important, whether in corporate life or on flights, to clearly define roles, responsibilities and rules of engagement. Otherwise chaos ensues.

"OK, let's review it one last time. In case of fire, you two girls get the hose, the Captain to my right will turn on the tap, and you tent-head at the back, sound the alarm."

BUSINESS TYCOONS AND EXECUTIVES

Like most little kids, you would have fantasized about growing up and sitting next to a senior corporate executive on a flight and getting that uber-leap in your career. Every professional has heard tales where careers were transformed over the course of a short flight. The MBA student who got a seat placement and thereby a job placement, with a senior executive. The corporate CEO, seated next to a business tycoon, who was offered a significant equity stake by the time they landed. The entrepreneur who convinced a hardnosed venture capitalist to invest a few million dollars over pretzels and juice.

If you are part of the rat race on the ground, you need to find the fat cats in the skies. Fat cats only travel business class so you will have to invest a significant chunk of your savings to fly along. Fat cats are morning people and you will never spot them on one of the 'lifestyle flights' (between noon and 4 pm), usually reserved for actors and models. Lastly, they have the attention span of mosquitoes on a nudist beach, so make the most of the minuscule window that you get to strike a conversation.

I have had the privilege of sitting next to various fat cats in the course of my 1,000-flight career. I haven't navigated the rat race any better though and I'm stuck where I have always been. And as I look back sadly upon all those flight opportunities that came my way, I am most wistful about the one bad takeoff that cost me a glowing career in fast-moving consumer goods marketing.

I had managed an upgrade to business on a Mumbai-Delhi flight. You can't get better than that for a fat cat sighting – business class on an early morning departure on the most popular travel sector for corporates. I used FIFO and quickly settled into my seat, waiting for a fat cat to meow.

A tall, strapping gentleman boarded and sat himself down next to me. Crisp white shirt, khaki trousers, exquisite shoes and a watch more avant-garde than the cockpit – the immaculate corporate executive. A couple of flunkies followed, wished him a pleasant flight and disappeared to economy. Whoever passed by gave him a respectful nod of acknowledgement. One or two stragglers walked across to say hello and offer a limp handshake.

"Who is he?" I was asking myself as I racked my brain furiously. I had seen him in the press but was finding it hard to place him. *"I think I have seen you somewhere,"* is the worst possible way to start a fat cat conversation; you probably have better chances of hitting it off if you fart loudly and then ask, *"Was that you?"*

Then my eyes latched onto a little logo on the pocket of his shirt. A blue 'U'. Of course, Hindustan Unilever – India's largest consumer goods and foods company and part of the worldwide Unilever group. The parent of brands such as Dove, Ponds, Lipton, Vaseline – the list could go on and on. And the gentleman was Nitin – the Chief Executive Officer. And I had just struck the mother cat of fat cats.

Even before takeoff, I was on cloud number nine. A switch from the boring world of financial services to the exciting world of foods and detergents suddenly seemed a few intelligent sentences away. So I wiped the sweat off my palms, combed down my hair, and prepared to start the most important conversation of my life.

The plane started rumbling down the runway with the jet engines firing at full capacity. It was a bit noisy in the cabin and I thought that I should maybe wait until we reached cruising altitude before I made my grand entry. The plane started climbing and I rehearsed my opening sentence over and over again. I was ready and raring to go.

Out of the clear blue, we hit an air pocket and the plane lurched. I shrieked and I gripped his hand tightly. As in, I only broke three of his knuckles. As I continued my wailing, most of the cabin looked at me in surprise. And even the attendants stood up to check what was happening.

Nitin graciously waited till the turbulence had passed and my shrieks had mellowed down to little whimpers. And as he extricated his hand from my vice-like clutches, he said in a stiff yet polite tone, *"Bumpy flight, isn't it?"* And he reached for his newspaper and read it till we landed.

I am still rat racing in financial services.

SINGLE AND ATTRACTIVE CO-PASSENGERS

If you are male, this section is probably moot because it is a well-observed fact that single women do not generally travel by plane. It's a little surprising actually because the airports are full of pretty women who appear to be single. They are alone in the coffee shops, or browsing through books in lonely bookstores, or standing wistfully on the moving walkways. But they never seem to board – it's as if there is a Bermuda triangle between the gate, aerobridge and plane that just sucks them in. Or possibly they bump into long-lost husbands or boyfriends at the gate and board with them. Or maybe they all come to the airport, change their mind and then take the train instead.

In any case, all women, irrespective of their relationship status, get seated on rows 21 through 25. It is standard check-in procedure to put them together so that they can surreptitiously check each other out with raised eyebrows, giving each other the ubiquitous woman-to-woman look over.

If you are female, this section is equally moot because it is a well-observed fact that attractive men do not generally travel by plane. It's a little surprising actually because the airports are full of attractive men who appear to be single. They are alone in the lounges, or at the airport bars, or standing wistfully at gates checking out the attendants. But they never seem to board – it's as if they decided that the cricket match on the TV at the gate was actually more important than the flight itself. Or possibly they fall into the urinals and come out disheveled and seeped in body odor. Or maybe they were all heading to the airport, but lost their way and as usual, refused to ask for directions.

That said, if the Boeing or Airbus gods, depending on who you pray to, do happen to seat you next to an unattached god or goddess, you have to make the most of it. If even a tinge of self-doubt creeps into your mind, remind yourself that you have two critical things going in your favor. It is an uncomfortable walk to the exit and even if he or she makes it there, it's a 38,000 foot drop to the ground. So there really is little choice for them but to listen to you.

"You probably get this all the time but you have the most beautiful elbows…"

So now that you have an attentive, and more importantly, captive audience of one, listed below are a sample of mind-blowing icebreakers that should have him or her breathlessly giving you a phone number, BlackBerry pin and email ID by the time the *"We will be landing shortly"* announcements come on.

- So where are you flying to?
- Have you ever flown before?
- Going home or on vacation?
- Can I borrow the newspaper?
- Hey! This newspaper has yesterday's news.
- You are classier than first class.
- How did a bomb like you get through security?
- It's true! Angels do fly!
- Was that the plane or did my heart just take off?
- Can I redeem some miles for some smiles?
- I hope this plane doesn't fall for you, like I have.
- In case it does fall, can I have your name and number for insurance purposes?

- I wish my boarding card had your photograph on it.
- Can you give me directions to wherever you are going?
- Lovely elbows. Do they run in the family?
- I missed the safety demo. How does one use this seat belt thingy?
- Do you prefer headwinds or tailwinds?
- They're out of blankets. But you can use me.
- Hey, want to cross the dateline together?
- Would you fancy a visit to Khandala?
- Hey, want to claim baggage together?
- Hey, want to walk down the aisle with me?
- Hi, I am SH891074532 on shaadi.com.
- I'm not very hungry. Shall we just share a meal tray?
- The food is a tad bland, isn't it? Shall I spice it up with some tadka?
- Shall I put this armrest up and we can get the party started?
- Do you want me to help you recline?

Once the ice has broken and melted, you can move on to in-flight games that should global warm the object of your affection even further. One of my favorite ones is 'Aisle Be Damned with Airport Codes'.

"I soooooo prefer Bingo. Two little ducklings quack on my back…."

Every airport in the world has a unique three-letter code – London Heathrow is LHR, Prague is PRG and so on. Hand her a list of all the 9,000+ airports with their corresponding codes and then ask her to decode the specific airports you name. Start by giving her something easy like:

Hanchey Army Heliport (USA) – In Amenas (Algeria) – Rishiri (Japan) – Thompson Robbins (USA)

And she will toss back her head and laugh when she decodes it to:

HEY – IAM – RIS – HEE

She should surely blush a beetroot red at:

Uralsk (Kazakhstan) – Monclova (Mexico) – Yelland (USA) – Galena (USA)

URA – LOV – ELY – GAL

And then raise it up a notch.

In Amenas (Algeria) – Fukuoka (Japan) – Lago Argentino (Argentina) – Alowe (Gabon) – Edmundo Barrios (Venezuela) – Innsbruck (Austria) – Hanscom Field (USA)

IAM – FUK – ING – AWE – SOM – INN – BED

It's a real fun game – at least I always seem to think so.

Having spent much of my social life in the air, I would have loved to write a chapter about all the great conversations I have had and the phone numbers I have received over the years. Unfortunately, I have but one.

It was a pleasant Mumbai-Delhi lifestyle flight and I had used one of my vouchers to upgrade myself to business. I was seated on the first row, looking out and charting a clear takeoff path for the pilot in my mind. An elderly lady came and sat next to me and her husband plonked himself across the aisle. He glanced at me and then came by and asked, *"Would you mind switching seats so I can sit with my wife?"* Ever the gentleman that I am, I stood up with a smile and walked across.

As I moved toward his seat, this stunning looking lady gave me a stunning looking glare through her stunning looking dark glasses. She was obviously a Bollywood actress, but not really being a films person, I couldn't place her. Her boarding card was lying on the armrest (she had, clearly, adopted BCP well) and as I sat down, I glanced at it – Raveena – one of the most popular Bollywood actresses in the '90s and early 2000s.

I guess I had a cheesy grin on my face because she glanced around the cabin, called the stewardess and asked, *"Aren't there any other empty seats available?"* There were none, but that quickly wiped any semblance of a smile off my face. It doesn't matter, I thought, as I picked up the paper and pretended to read, my mind racing on how to start a conversation.

What does one talk to a Bollywood actress about? Films, I would think. So I started racking my brains for the titles of her films I liked. But for the life of me, I couldn't recall the title of any film that she had acted in (did I mention that I am not really into movies?). The only thing I could vividly recall was this dance sequence from a movie where she was gyrating in the rain in a translucent yellow sari; I was a teenager at that time, so one can't really blame me for having that firmly imprinted in my memory. But two decades hence, it just didn't seem to be an appropriate conversation starter.

It had been 30 minutes since takeoff, time was running out and I hadn't even turned the newspaper page. Let's forget the past, I thought, and let me focus on the future. I was under the impression that she hadn't been acting lately and *"Raveena, it would be great to have you back in films"* would be a really classy icebreaker.

So I cleared my throat, had a swig of water, and prepared to deliver my *coup de grâce* when self-doubt struck. What if she says, *"Thanks, which film of mine did you particularly like?"* And I would hem and haw, trying to avoid talking about her rain dances. Or what if she was currently acting in films and I was just unaware. That would be a total disaster – her watching in disdain as I struggle to take my foot out of my mouth. So I went back to the newspaper as I scrambled to sort out this latest conundrum in my confused mind.

In the meanwhile, she asked the attendant for a blanket and wrapped it around herself. And she called for a pillow and placed it under her neck. And she removed her sunglasses and laid them delicately on the armrest. And noting the torture that I was going through, she turned to me and with the classiest look and politest tone asked, *"Do you mind if I put the window shade down?"* And in my deepest bedroom voice, I stuttered, *"Ummmm... not at all."*

And she pulled down the shade, closed her eyes and slept all the way to landing.

And I am still rat racing in singledom.

But look, it's okay to make mistakes as long as you learn from them. And I surely don't want any of you to suffer the same fate that I did with Raveena. So here's a helpful Bollywood actress conversation cheatsheet that I have prepared. I suggest you use this handy template and replicate this with whoever it is you'd like to sit next to on a flight.

RISHI'S CHEATSHEET FOR BOLLYWOOD ACTRESSES AS FLIGHT COMPANIONS

1. Name of Bollywood Flight Companion: Katrina

Awesome opening sentence: *"Hi Katrina, I'm Rishi. Kya aap mere saath hindi mein vartalaap karna chahengi?"* (Would you like to converse with me in Hindi?)

Favorite movie: *Singh is Kinng* (Singh is the King)

Why you liked the movie: *"Amazing acting by you. Just amazing."*

Other discussion items: Mention that you stayed in the same apartment complex and stalked the elevators for two years but never saw her. Does she only take the stairs?

2. Name of Bollywood Flight Companion: Amisha

Awesome opening sentence: *"Hi, Amisha, I'm Rishi. So does that make us a Mishi Rishi? Lol!"*

Favorite movie: *Kaho na pyar hai* (Tell Me There Is Love)

Why you liked the movie: *"Brilliant acting by you. Just brilliant."*

Other discussion items: Remind her that you went to the same school and that you seriously contemplated flunking a couple of years so that you could end up in her batch.

3. Name of Bollywood Flight Companion: Preity

Awesome opening sentence: *"Hi Preity, I'm Rishi. Try saying this real fast – Pretty Preity prays with proper Piparaiya"*

Favorite movie: *Kal ho na ho* (There May or May Not Be a Tomorrow)

Why did you like the movie: *"Fantastic acting by you. Just fantastic."*

Other discussion items: Tell her that when the wind blows past her cute dimples, airplanes encounter turbulence.

A MILE-HIGH THREESOME

But sometimes you may just hit the jackpot, the mother lode of jackpots, and get to participate in a mile-high threesome. As yours truly was fortunate enough to on a recent flight.

I boarded and made my way to my usual aisle seat. The plane was packed, and the cabin was peopled primarily by corporate executives and a surprisingly large number of tattooed backpackers. A smartly dressed individual sat next to me, and I returned his smile with the condescending look reserved for centre-seat occupants.

As we settled in with our respective reading material, a beautiful young lady murmured an excuse me and we both promptly stepped aside to let her pass– damn, it was one of those times when you wish you had the centre spot. As we sunk back into our seats, I could have sworn his smile was broader than before. And wasn't he smooth? Even before the flight had taken off, he had broken the ice, and I couldn't help but hear snippets of their scintillating conversation.

He: *So what do you do?*

She: *I'm with (a leading media house). Heading sales.*

He: *Wow, that's quite something. You handle sales for the*

entire country.

She: *Yes, the whole of India. One business vertical.*

The conversation moved to education, and he had just the appropriate words of admiration for her yaddayadda tale about being the first graduate in her family.

He: *I'm passionate about education as well. In fact, I want to start a venture fund that invests in education.*

She: *That is so noble. You totally should.*

He: *I will take ideas from you.*

She: *Absolutely! Anytime!*

They spoke about holidays, flights, upbringings, movies, past jobs and so on, the conversation getting increasingly animated as it progressed. Throughout, she sat, legs crossed towards him, shoe dangling, holding his eye, and with a finger twirling through her hair like a chopstick through ramen. He was reciprocating –brushing a hand through his hair and puffing out his chest. It was a fascinating study in mating behavior.

He: *So, do you speak Hindi?*

She: *Well I can.*

He: *So say a few words.*

She (blushing): *Well I can't really speak shudh Hindi.*

And they both laughed heartily, like long-lost pals reunited after a handful of Kumbhs.

As the food trolley rolled in around 30 minutes into the flight, he introduced himself.

"Hi, I'm Suresh."

"I am Priya."

I started visualizing 'Priya weds Suresh' wedding cards and a baraat led by a white horse and me. I was paying close attention by now, this being far more interesting than the 2011 Costa Book of the Year that I was plodding through.

"Sir, will you have the dhokla or the keemapav?" asked the hostess, interrupting our auditory threesome. He chose the dhokla, as did I.

"Do you have fruit?" she asked.

"I'm sorry, ma'am."

"Just give me a few sachets of milk powder then."

"Umm... sure."

And the hostess handed out a few. "I will be back with tea and coffee later."

"No thanks, just the milk powder is fine."

We were intrigued. "Why do you want these sachets?" he asked with flirtatious incredulity.

"Oh, my five-year-old daughter loves them. My husband and I love to see the faces she makes as she struggles with the powder gluing her mouth."

I choked on my dhokla. He probably did too. Because the conversation ended. Quite as abruptly as this chapter.

CLEARED TO LAND

"Flying is the second greatest thrill
known to man.... Landing is the first."
— Anonymous

You have successfully made it back to terra firma and the flight has pulled up to the gate. However, do not as yet, stand at ease. Some of the hardest work begins once the flight is completed.

TRANSIT PASSENGERS

Catching a connecting flight is one of the most stressful activities known to man. As you are transiting through any airport, you experience the phenomenon of time-space distanciation, where the space between gates increases as the time that you have compresses.

"Papa, let's play Hide and Seek, Papa. What do you mean no, Papa? Count to ten... Here I go, Papa... Wheeee!"

According to a recent survey, Indians have the best record in making their flight connections. And that is because a majority of them have learnt how to make transiting the airline's problem, thanks to a little contraption called the wheelchair.

Shortly before landing, *desi* aunty is distressed to experience an attack of deep vein thrombosis or any other difficult-to-pronounce medical condition that render her stocky legs useless. Then as she explains the poignant situation to the attendant, she keeps the most pitiful face on till she gets a *"Do not worry Madam, we will have a wheelchair waiting for you at the gate"*.

Once the airline gets her onto a wheelchair, it is now their headache. They will rush through queues, take the shortest of shortcuts and honk their way to the connecting gate in double quick time. Aunty just sits back and admires the scenery as it whizzes by.

The challenge is for poor *desi* uncle who gets a nice workout, jogging alongside at a steady pace.

IMMIGRATION

Immigration can be the biggest bottleneck in your entire journey and the more developed the nation that you have landed in, the longer it will take to clear immigration. So as soon as the aircraft doors open, run like Forrest Gump being chased by Usain Bolt.

Hurdle over suitcases and food trolleys. Overtake as many people as possible between the plane and the immigration counters.

As you reach the immigration area, you will encounter two queues. One for nationals of that country and the other for foreigners. If you have landed in your country, your queue will be longer. If you have landed in a foreign country, the foreigners' queue will be longer.

The decision tree will further branch out into a short queue and a long queue, and of course, you will choose the short one. Over the next 15 minutes, you notice that the long queue is moving much faster and you soon comprehend why. One immigration officer is servicing the short queue while four are servicing the long one. Although it is too late now to switch queues, so you just bite your lip and stay on.

As you near the immigration counter, one of the four officers from the long queue comes to powwow with the sole officer in your short one. And your officer drops everything, leans back and starts chitchatting. And they go on for a while, discussing the latest goings-on in the scandalous world of immigration.

Once they have mutually concluded as to which counter is sleeping with which counter, the short queue starts to move again. Soon you have reached the little yellow line which signals your impending rendezvous with the sole immigration officer. You excitedly stand with both feet firmly behind the line, lest a laser beam from the ceiling were to slice off any toe that accidently crosses it. You wait till he is free and then gingerly walk up to him with a pasted smile on your face.

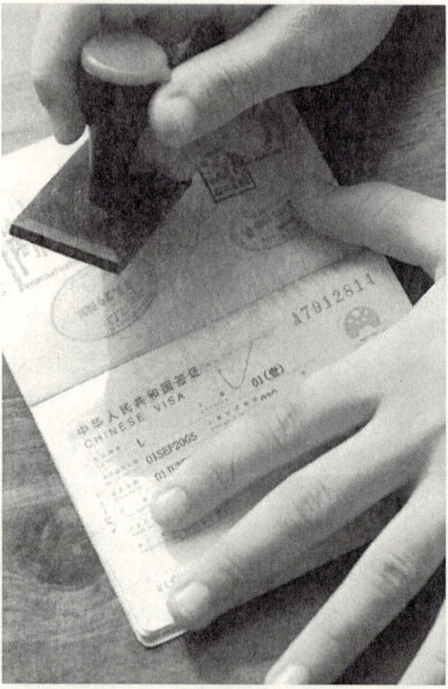

"Damn man, you are so ugly,
I'm going to waive the photograph requirement."

Without looking up, he will hold out his palm where you will politely place your passport and immigration form. He will languidly open your passport, look at the photograph, look at you, then look back at the photograph. You can see the nuts and bolts in his brain rasping, straining to draw some correlation to the grotesque face in the photograph and the pasted smile standing in front of him, but there is none. You may as well have been on the interplanetary space bus from Jupiter that landed at gate number 12. He lets it go though – it's not the right time or place to empathize with you on the shortcomings of your gene pool.

He will then swipe your passport through a machine on his desk and $1.99 discreetly gets charged to your credit card toward the Immigration Officers Welfare Fund.

"How long are you here for? Why? Where are you staying?"

These are the standard questions and you should answer them with an illiterate look. Nothing works better than a confused, non English-speaking, heavy accented tone to exasperate most immigration officers in countries across the world.

"How much money are you carrying?"

This is a trick question. I usually answer *"a few hundred euros"* but was once asked to prove it by emptying my wallet. Out tumbled fourteen euros and an optimistically stashed but since long expired, condom packet. A Platinum MasterCard came to the rescue else I was all prepared to warm the aisle seat on the next flight back.

Don't chew gum, don't look guilty and keep phones off while you are at the counter. Nothing pisses off an immigration officer more than a loud shrill ring with Aunty Rupalben on the other end, welcoming you to Southall. Don't make conversation, don't ask about ground transportation options and don't stay back to say thank you. Just wait till the rubber stamp goes 'thupp' on your passport and scram.

If you do plan to make the transition to illegal alien status, ensure that you are not carrying any incriminating souvenirs from the humdrum life that you are hoping to leave behind. They may check your bags and finding *'All the best for your new life. Do not get deported!'* farewell cards will not help your case.

BAGGAGE CLAIM

You then get into the drudgery of retrieving baggage. You dash your way to the concerned carousel, picking up a baggage trolley along the way and wait patiently for it to start. And as the belt starts revolving with a creak, the old nursery rhyme starts playing in your head. *"The wheels of the bus go round and round, round and round, round and round..."*

Bags start appearing one by one, and you wait for your Samsonite to emerge. You pray that the first suitcase on the belt be yours, but Erma Bombeck debunked one of aviation's long-standing hoaxes by discovering that the first piece of luggage belongs to no one. It's just a dummy suitcase to give everyone hope. Your heart sinks as people around you lift their bags and ride into the sunset. And you are still standing, eyes transfixed at little plastic curtains at both ends of the belt, through which bags magically appear and disappear.

If you are bored, readjust any heavy suitcase such that half of it is now sticking out of the belt. It is great fun to hear the screams as it circles around, knocking kneecaps one after the other.

You should park the trolley facing away from the belt so that you can accelerate immediately, without having to maneuver through the throngs around you. Once your bags arrive, scoop them onto the trolley and zoom away, as your fellow conveyor-waiters look at you admiringly.

If your bags haven't arrived, let me extinguish any vestiges of hope that are burning in the candle-stand of your feeble heart. Give up, you ding bag loser. There is a popular scientific theory that the rings of Saturn are made up entirely of lost airline luggage so that's where your junk will probably end up. Count your blessings that this indispensable book was part of your carry-on baggage and that your jacket, if you have followed my advice, is thankfully not in Italy.

"I'll be damned, I left behind that lips, hips and tips book on the flight as well…"

CUSTOMS

This is the final frontier of your airport experience before you are thrown at the mercy of ground transportation. Here is where a posse of serious looking dogs, men and women check your baggage for unauthorized substances, food items, valuables and the like. If you don't have packets of heroin stashed in your rectum, crocodile skins in the false bottom of your luggage, or an African parrot sedated in your shaving kit, you should be fine.

The innocent people, however, seem to exhibit the most guilt as they pass through customs. The best way to clear customs is to sport a 'busy person who is slightly lost' look. Push your trolley with one hand and keep glancing at the watch on the other. Squint at the various signs around you and let out an audible sigh of recognition when you see the green 'Nothing to Declare' sign overhead.

"What drugs? I'm just checking out the lingerie."

You may encounter the occasional whacko like the Japanese customs official who decided to test Rover by hiding a pack of marijuana in a random suitcase, circling a conveyor belt at Narita, Tokyo. Rover apparently wasn't the most capable sniffer dog in Japan, showing greater promise in urinating on hydrants. His handler, Numskull-san, unfortunately didn't help matters either by forgetting which suitcase he had hidden the cannabis in. Last we heard, frantic announcements were being made asking any drug-carrying passengers to identify themselves to the authorities.

Simply look through any customs officials glancing in your direction – you are well beyond the days when you used to engage in petty smuggling. If you hear an *"Excuse me"*, ignore it and keep walking. If you hear a whistle, wiggle your little finger inside your ear and flick out some wax.

You should only stop if you feel a set of 42 canine teeth chomping out a chunk of your bum. Or if you sense the cold steely pressure of an officer's semi-automatic pistol against your temple.

TOURIST TAX REFUND

While on the topic of customs, I think it's appropriate that I finally blow the lid off, Snowden-style, one of the most closely guarded governmental secrets of all time.

After one of the numerous global financial crises – no one is sure which – the International Monetary Fund (IMF) called for a top-secret meeting of the finance ministers of its 188 member countries. The single-point agenda: how to jump-start the global economy by swindling its people. As is usually the case in any committee-type forum, no one really wanted to publicly accept that they don't have a problem gypping the citizens of their own country. So they came up with a game plan in which each government would defraud the citizens of other nations. And thus was born the Tourist Refund Scheme.

Tourists traveling abroad engage in essentially the same few activities: taking photographs of popular attractions, enjoying the local cuisine and visiting strip clubs. Many of them also do a lot of shopping. The tax refund scheme, prevalent in many countries around the world, allows tourists to claim a refund on all the sales or value added taxes that they have paid on their purchases in the country abroad. This is done by submitting a form, which is to be stamped by customs at the airport just before they leave the foreign country.

The IMF plan was for governments to encourage tourists to shop by promising a tax refund and then making it impossible for them to actually claim the refund. So they developed the following rules that all countries had to abide by:

- Department stores will display attractive posters promising *Easy and Instant Tax Refund for Tourists.* These posters are a complete lie.

- You, as a tourist, will have to present your passport when you go shopping to receive a tax refund form from the store.

- If you do receive a form, you will have to complete multiple copies of the form in the local language. If the local language is English, you will have to complete the form in Braille.

- If you do fill the form, you will have to get the form stamped by customs before you leave the country, at a special Tax Refund counter hidden somewhere within the airport.

- To locate the counter, you could ask the airport information desk. They do, however, have strict instructions to feign complete ignorance and point tourists to Starbucks instead.

- If you do get directed to Starbucks, go blow up 6 dollars on some venti-grande-doppio shitshat.

- If you do reach the counter through sheer good luck, the customs official will stamp the form only after visually inspecting the purchased items. Given that you've already checked in, your merchandise is probably already with your checked-in bags. So the only tax refund you are eligible for is on the new Victoria's Secret bra or Calvin Klein briefs that you are wearing. And it is quite debatable whether the refund amount is worth the peek-a-boo that you will have to engage in.

- If you do get the form stamped, you will have to

shove it into a small postage-paid envelope that will be provided to you.

- If you do mail the envelope, do so with the knowledge that no one knows where those envelopes go. My guess is Rovaniemi, Finland – the home of Santa Claus, where he burns them in the fireplace along with the letters of all those pesky little kids who want Christmas gifts.

I hope you understand, there is nothing in life such as a tax refund. Taxes only travel one way: from you to *them.*

"Go on your tippy toes… tippy toes, dude…
I still don't see that damn Tax Refund counter."

PERFECT AIRPORT PICKUPS

"We're perfect. I timed this out so we would pull up at the terminal exactly 17 minutes after their flight is supposed to land. That gives them just enough time to get off the plane, pick up their bags and be walking out of the terminal as we roll up. I tell you, it's a thing of beauty. I cannot express to you the feeling I get from a perfect airport pickup."

— George to Kramer, as they head to pick up Jerry and Elaine from the airport, in the sitcom *Seinfeld.*

If your IQ is above the half century mark, you would have researched the cheapest ways to travel from the airport and would comfortably be on the metro, bus or train to city central. Many people however, prefer to take a taxicab into a new city. They might as well be holding a large sign engraved with, 'Come Fleece Me'.

AIRPORT TAXIS

Airport taxis, all over the world, are accustomed to ripping off passengers. It's part of the arrivals ritual. Whether taking the longest routes, using fixed meters, charging absurd rates, pressing buttons that add dollars to the fare – every trick has been perfected by the global taxi trade. Initially, I tried to fight it and would argue with the cabbies, threaten to call the cops and note down their license numbers but to no avail.

So I decided, if you can't beat them, join them.

Before I travel to a new city, I research what the taxi fare should be from the airport to my destination. I then bump it up by a reasonable 20% rip-off margin. If a taxi driver has been waiting in airport queues for hours on end, with the sole objective of picking up an unsuspecting tourist, I think he deserves a reasonable rate-up over the actual fare. So I mentally incorporate that in my calculations.

"Welcome! Let me be the first one to take you for a ride."

I take a taxi and reach my destination. If the fare he is charging me is within the 20% rip-off margin amount, I graciously pay and leave. However, if he has dared to charge me more than that, I execute my 'Rip-Off the Rip-Off' strategy. I pull out item 11 on my essential packing list – a stink bomb (available in most toy stores around the world), pay the tab, defuse it, quietly shove it under the seat and leave. If you are concerned about roaming in strange countries armed with stink bombs, you can as easily unwrap a packet of smelly blue cheese and leave it in the cab. Rest assured, the cab will not have another passenger for the next few days.

It is satisfying, ripping off the ripper off-ers.

THE PRE-BOOKED CAR SERVICE

If you feature in the 'About Us' section of your company's website, it means that you are somewhat professionally relevant and possibly eligible for a pre-booked car service. Theoretically, in most countries, it should be a pleasure to experience this luxury. A smart gentleman with a prominent placard waits for you as close to the arrivals gate as is regulatorily possible. He tips his cap upon seeing you, dives to help with your baggage and leads the way to the car park where he has parked in the most prominent spot. He puts your luggage in a spacious boot, hands you the newspaper and a bottle of chilled water and then a Jaguar purrs to life.

In emerging markets, it turns out to be a slightly different experience. As the plane lands and moves toward its gate, you switch on your phone. The first message you receive is from your phone company, advising you of roaming charges in that city. And then your phone goes berserk with missed call alerts from a number that you don't recognize. That's the number of the chauffeur who is there to receive you.

His *modus operandi* is simple. He is in the parking lot, playing cards with his friends. Every few seconds, he picks up his mobile phone and dials your number to check whether you have landed. If the call fails to go through, he carries on with his game. The minute he hears a ring on the other side, he yells *"Pack!"*, flings the cards and dashes to Arrivals.

If you are expecting him to be waiting at Arrivals with a prominent name placard, you will be sadly disappointed. He will be carrying a little sheet of paper, crumpled in his hip pocket, which will have everything spelt incorrectly in a light grey color pencil.

'JOURNAL ALECTRICK WELCOMES JOCK WELSH'

Chances are that you will walk up and down a few times before you notice this little scribbling. Do not be impatient. You would have seen many names on other placards that you recognize and Arrivals is a great place to catch up with acquaintances from the past.

When you find him, hiding in the furthermost corner of the pickup area, you can yell *"Found you!"* and give him a hug. That's culturally acceptable in an airport 'picker-pickee' relationship in most countries. He will not help with your bags and instead raise an eyebrow for making him wait so long. Quietly follow as he marches to the end of the parking lot where an indigenous automobile from the Beatles era awaits you. Grab the paper that has doubled as the floor mat and enjoy the read as you get bounced all the way to your hotel.

THE AIRPORT PICKUP

"Shit guys, I think we got the wrong placards. Where are the 'Welcome Aunt Thelma!' signs that we made?"

If you get saddled with the duty of picking up someone from an airport, the objective should be to execute the perfect airport pickup described earlier. In case you do botch it and reach earlier than the flight, grab a nice spot, pick up a can of soda and get ready for a lovely evening of people watching.

It is fascinating to observe travelers as they come out of airports with twinkling eyes and tired faces. The executives and hitchhikers march purposefully to ground transportation without batting an eyelid. And the rest of the folks scan the masses of waiting faces, searching for their loved ones who have come to receive them. And it is quite something to observe the waves of emotions that are exhibited when they spot each other. Shrieks, tears, kisses, laughs, smiles – time flies as you watch family after family hugging each other; couple after couple leaping into each other's arms. Oh, the sentimental reunions that happen at the meeting point outside Arrivals.

Oh forget it! Writing emotional drama is obviously not my forte. Visualize yourself as an ace photographer in charge of creating the 'Women at Mumbai airport' calendar and find 12 real world models amongst all the people there, to adorn the pages of your imaginary calendar. And as you mentally click a head shot of Miss August, and a side profile of Miss September, you turn around and damn, there is your mother-in-law, waddling out of Arrivals.

AND THEY FLEW HAPPILY EVER AFTER

And so that finally brings us to the end of our journey. Set your bags down in the bedroom, inspect the damage caused to the zippers and wheels, and yank out all the stickers and tags that have been attached to the luggage handles. Put any unused foreign currency in the travel pouch, your passport beneath the underwear in the first drawer, and save your boarding cards as proof just in case the frequent flier miles don't get credited.

Now would also be an opportune moment to pull out the last item on the packing list – a smartphone or tablet – and tweet praises for this book.

Just loved reading #AisleBeDamned by @RishiPiparaiya. Hee Hee Hee... it's sooo funny that my stomach hurts. Need some #churan

Starting from the trolley at Departures all the way up to your taxi at Arrivals, I trust I have added value to every aspect of your flying experience. And just imagine, all this for lesser than the price of an airport sandwich!

And guess what, I so appreciate the whopping 15 rupees (25 cents) that I am earning from you on this copy, that I am throwing in a bonus chapter, specially for you.

COMMERCE, LITERATURE AND ZEN

"You haven't seen a tree until you've seen its shadow from the sky."
— Amelia Earhart

It wasn't so starkly apparent to me until I wrapped up this wrap-up chapter: I am truly multifaceted.

PIPARAIYA ON ZEN

At some point, we have all asked ourselves the fundamental existential question: *What is life?*

Mathematically speaking, if the number of takeoffs you have made equals the number of landings you have made, you are alive. If the number of takeoffs unfortunately exceeds the number of landings, you are dead.

My condolences in that case and I hope you had adequate life insurance. When I am not flying, writing, daydreaming or updating my résumé, I am actually peddling some awesome insurance products. So google me, brush away the electronic dust gathered on my LinkedIn profile and send me a mail. I will ensure that you get adequately covered.

Put *'David Guetta'* as the subject of your mail. No particular reason – that just happens to be whom I am listening to as I write this paragraph.

"You shoot me down, but I won't fall. I am titanium..."

Mind-blowing!

But maybe you are not titanium and in that case you must be wondering: *Who am I?* Let me help you answer that.

Please take as much time as needed, but I sincerely request that you give honest responses to the following:

1. Would you rather have –

   A. Miles

   B. Bones

2. Would you rather –

   A. Face travel blackout dates

   B. Sleep in a kennel

3. Would you rather –

   A. Reach Platinum status for no tangible benefits

   B. Play fetch for a yummy biscuit

If you have primarily answered A's, you are a loyal frequent flier program member. If you have largely answered B's, you are a cocker spaniel.

Speaking of frequent flier programs, I am way beyond this silver, gold and platinum tier shitshat. The periodic table actually doesn't have any metal that exemplifies my aristocratic status. I am at like, Kryptonite tier. At Kryptonite tier, airlines don't give me miles to fly with them; they offer me equity stakes.

"Hmmm... It's not a bad offer: 4% in preferred stock, a Board seat and a private lavatory whenever I fly."

PIPARAIYA ON PHILOSOPHY

You think you've gone through stressful periods in life? *Oh really?* What happened? Your business failed? You got divorced? The bank repossessed your house? They've named a medical condition after you?

I have gone through and survived eight months with just one remaining blank page in my passport. So don't talk to me about stress, Jeezball!

PIPARAIYA ON ECONOMICS

The cheapest New York-Mumbai round trip air ticket in 1992 was approximately $900. The cheapest ticket for the same sector in 2012 (20 years later) was $1100. Oil in 1992 was $18 a barrel. Oil in 2012 was $110 a barrel.

Here is a completely radical theory on why the airline industry doesn't make money: I believe there is something wrong with their pricing model.

(Dear Nobel Committee, I anyway need to visit Sweden this year to buy some doorknobs at IKEA. My schedule permitting, I could swing by your office to collect the Nobel Prize for Economics around that time).

"Yes, I am extremely honored and cannot adequately express my gratitude to Sweden. Just imagine, if not for them, I may never have been able to open doors again."

Speaking of economics, the world can make all the India versus China comparisons that it wants. But I'll be damned if India is not making significantly more progress in all spheres.

Take infrastructure for example – the government is building an ambitious air corridor at 41,000 feet, connecting Mumbai and Delhi. It should be ready within the next three years and will cut the 95-minute flight time by as much as 20 minutes. It is a fantastic example of public-private partnership and various global conglomerates have expressed keen interest in bidding for the project.

Discussions on how to operate tollbooths at 41,000 feet are still underway.

Speaking of China, do they manufacture planes in China? Because while I can live with the shoddy toys and flimsy garments, I would be seriously concerned about flying in anything that has a 'Made in China' sticker.

PIPARAIYA ON TECHNOLOGY

The global telecommunications industry is growing at an incredible pace – mobile subscriptions having tripled in the past five years to six billion. Global telecom companies made capital expenditures of over $300 billion in 2011. In that same year, global telecom service providers earned revenues equal to India's GDP – $1.8 trillion.

Boeing and Airbus alone employ over 200,000 professionals, a majority of them scientists and engineers, who file over 1,000 new patents annually. Their combined research and development budget is upward of $5 billion per annum. A modern 747 has 274 km of wiring, six million parts and enough computing horsepower that allows the plane to virtually fly itself, like magic.

On a completely unrelated note, no one has still been able to figure out how to stop mobile phones from interfering with an airplane's systems.

PIPARAIYA ON CAPITALISM

I have had the privilege of traveling on practically all the major airlines in the world. Flying in economy and business and once, even in first class. And while there are a lot of fantastic airlines out there, there is one particular airline that has got just about every aspect of the experience right.

Customer service is impeccable, flights are rarely delayed, food and entertainment is top notch, the flight crew seemingly handpicked from the ramps of Milan and Paris, and much of their fleet still has that desirable 'new plane smell' in the cabin.

If you are a seasoned traveler, you probably have already guessed which airline I am referring to. And if you haven't yet had the pleasure of flying with them, book your next trip now. Trust an expert: you will not regret it.

Kudos to the team at (insert airline name) Airways. Well done, you folks absolutely ROCK!

(Dear Airline CEOs – I don't really enjoy doing this, but finances are a tad tight and the blank space is available for sale to the highest bidder. If cash flow is an issue for you, as I imagine it could be, we can discuss bartering complimentary lifetime business class tickets for me and my buddies).

"Going once, going twice, gone! To Africa Airways. For two acres of rice fields, a hundred heads of cattle, and some multi-colored beads."

PIPARAIYA ON MARKETING

Even the structures, properties and reactions of carbon-based compounds are probably more interesting than the boring poppycock that features in the in-flight magazines. So the airlines may as well replace the magazines with organic chemistry textbooks. At least the average IQ of the passengers will increase a few points between takeoff and landing.

Alternatively, please visit *www.aislebedamned.com,* go to its online coffee shop, and vote for airlines to offer this book as in-flight reading material. If I get 1,000 votes, I will recruit a marketing serf to hound airlines. If I get 10,000 votes, I will also contest the next parliamentary elections.

I am particularly hopeful that unconventional aviation business gurus such as Sir Richard Branson will appreciate my genius and place the first bulk orders.

Now look Richie, can I call you Richie, this is what we can do. I can customize the cover for you and help you select who among your team should feature on it. For that, I will need to sit on the aisle seat on about 40 Mumbai-London-Mumbai Virgin Atlantic flights, but I can live with that. If I am making 40 round trips on your airline, I will probably come up with some more cool anecdotes and I will include them exclusively in your edition. I can also replace page numbers with the Virgin logo; numerals are anyway irrelevant on a gripping page-turner such as this.

Now you will probably want a customized title as well, and knowing you, it will have to be racy. How about

‘Swaying Hips by the Aisle Seats’? Nice, huh? I thought so. In what will become a business school case study of how a nobody has increased his negotiating power with a multi-billionaire, I have already registered *www.swayinghips.com*. Smart, huh? I can offer it to you to make a really cool website. And we can also launch a line of co-branded ‘Swaying Hips of a Virgin’ merchandise – tees, calendars, lingerie, home furnishings, etc.

We will keep all this under wraps and then grandly announce it at a mid-air press conference aboard a Virgin Atlantic flight. The tabloids will sit in first class, the mainstream media in business, and the financial journalists in economy. Ha! Our respective press interviews will then be followed by a mid-air fashion show down the aisle, keeping in line with the swaying hips theme.

What say, Branny boy! Let’s go for it!

PIPARAIYA ON FOREIGN POLICY

Speaking of the parliament, I may just have a very bright future in the government. I believe that I would be fabulous in international relations, for example.

For starters, there would be few parliamentarians who have flown as much as I have. That itself makes me a natural choice for the post. Add to that my unique ability to acquire accents – a Qantas plane as much as flies above my head and I can start speaking in Australian. And finally, imagine how cool it would be – walking into a bar and introducing oneself as the Minister of External Affairs (wink).

It will be a stressful job though; I mean, just take our immediate neighbors. It was purely unintentional but something tells me that I may have already pissed off China. I do not think Nepal is going to give me a medal of honor anytime soon. I have never visited Bangladesh but was impressed to learn that 10% of its GDP comes from agriculture, 20% from services and 70% from restaurants whose menus masquerade as Indian cuisine. I believe we have a neighbor Bhutan, which measures Gross National Happiness; I will probably have to hold hands and skip with my Bhutanese counterpart on state visits. I am always on a first name basis with anyone from Sri Lanka, neither of us being able to pronounce the other's last name. And Pakistan will be particularly tricky – getting them to remove their air pockets from our skies will be my first order of business.

Speaking of Pakistan, is it just our borders that are disputed or does the disagreement extend to the airspace as well? I understand the whole 'barbed-wire fencing on the ground' concept but how do countries mark out their airspace? Are there ropes strung across the sky?

"Cross this side and I am going to peck each of your freaking feathers off, you goddamn son of a swallow."

PIPARAIYA ON HARMONY

Speaking of borders, imagine a world without visas. No social classifications of business or tourist visitor or man-made barriers of single or multiple entries. You could just get out of bed and fly to any country, whenever you wish. And you could live there if you wanted to. And you could work there if someone valued your skills. And you could marry there if you found true love. And your children would be global citizens – getting a visa to *one earth* upon arrival. And consulates would only exist to promote art, culture and food festivals.

Just imagine this beautiful planet of ours – without borders and without visas.

(Dear Nobel Committee, I am on a roll, aren't I? Please bubble-wrap my Peace Prize along with the Economics one. And while I recognize that it is not in your preferred 'non-rhyming poems' genre, do consider awarding this awesome book, the Nobel Prize for Literature. While they should be pleased with the duo, three Nobels in a year will make Mom and Dad very proud indeed).

PIPARAIYA ON LITERATURE

And that is not to say that I can't write deep poetry that one struggles to interpret.

The celerity of man, oh, when will he learn? Affrighted are the valkyries waltzing on the clouds.

Speaking of writing, I don't know who drafts the scripts for the on-board announcements made by flight attendants. I can't really comment on international airlines but the words and phrases that they use in India are probably from the third century BC. I am serious. *Vilambh. Nishedh. Madira.* What language are they speaking in and what the heck are they saying?

"Dearly beloved, business is booming. Just won a mandate to script all pilot announcements for India Airways."

PIPARAIYA ON LOVE

If one can look beyond the smoke and mirrors that life presents, all of us really have the same intrinsic aspiration. To be able to someday redeem the '50% companion discount' airline voucher that has come in the mail.

"The world shall know this as a symbol of our eternal love…"

I know you are not going to believe it, but I swear to you that this truly happened. I was sitting on my aisle seat, concentrating on my laptop and peacefully minding my own business. Suddenly this gorgeous flight attendant appears next to me and gently lifts my spectacles from the bridge of my nose with a *"Sir, you have been working too hard"*. She then proceeds to pull out a wet tissue from her pocket and without using her wrists, just the momentum generated from an anti-clockwise rotation of her waist, she cleans the lenses to perfection.

I immediately switched loyalties to that airline, until the quarter in which it went bankrupt. Give me clean eyewear over a healthy balance sheet any day.

Note to that attendant: Please connect with me if you happen to be reading this. I have been contemplating LASIK for a while now, but the only thought stopping me, is you.

While the men from Mars, women from Venus theories may apply to typical couples, I am confident that a civilian-flight attendant combination will never face any communication gaps.

"Rishi calling sweetheart. Rishi calling sweetheart. Sweetheart, I will see you at the movies, ETA nineteen hundred hours. To get here, take two-two right heading zero-five-zero, from the

north-east entrance."

"Roger, dear. Did you manage to get good seats?"

"Affirmative, angel. Snagged two aisle seats at the back of the theatre."

"Copy, stud muffin. Shall we skip meal service after the video presentation? I feel fat."

"Negative, pumpkin, my coochie-woochie-sugar-poochie. We have a dinner reservation at Crazy Noodles under my name, Piparaiya. That's Papa-India-Papa-Alfa-Romeo-Alfa-India-Yankee-Alfa."

"Ten four, punky monkey. That sounds super. Over and out."

Do you think a couple such as this would ever have a reason to fight?

SIR, WHERE SHALL WE STACK THESE?

Now that I have so skillfully straddled such varied subjects and genres, I cannot help but wonder. How will bookstores categorize this book?

Is it fiction? Non-fiction?

Reference book? Picture book?

Humor? Horror?

Romance? Fantasy?

Travel? Philosophy?

Self-help? Severe dementia?

AND IN CONCLUSION . . .

"There is not much to say about most airplane journeys. Anything remarkable must be disastrous, so you define a good flight by negatives: you didn't get hijacked, you didn't crash, you didn't throw up, you weren't late, you weren't nauseated by the food. So you're grateful."

— Paul Theroux, *The Old Patagonian Express*

I believe that air travel is a lot more complex than it should be. I mean, can you imagine anyone pontificating for 200 pages on bus or train rides? We desperately need to simplify the overall flight experience.

There should be just two categories of air passengers – the 'Advance Bookers' and the 'Just Show Ups'. Given the value proposition, most people would probably fall in the 'Just Show Up' category.

If you are a Just Show Up-er, you will simply arrive at the airport with your bags and stroll from gate to gate. The information board at each gate will display the destination of the next flight, the departure time and the price of the ticket. The ticket price is dynamic, based on how many seats are still empty and how much time is left for departure. The airline will be flying with empty seats anyway – the more desperate it is to get passengers, the cheaper the ticket will be.

Based on your budget and locational preferences (beach, hills, family visit, etc.), you will get onto a plane of your choice. You will be offered last-minute hotel deals in the destination city so that accommodation is organized before you land. You drop off your bags at the gate and a little GPS chip gets attached to each one so that it will never get lost.

It is free seating and all seats come equipped with a seat belt, life vest, air bag, parachute and water bottle. An ultra low-cost vagabond class has been added where seating is modeled on the rides at amusement parks. Essentially, long communal benches where a little mechanical guardrail folds down and locks into place once the plane starts moving.

If you are an Advance Booker, you will get some fantastic benefits for the extra bucks that you have doled out. A week before your flight you can go online to view photographs of the airline's cabin crew and vote on who should be rostered for your flight. Résumés of pilots will also be displayed and you can choose to fly with whoever you feel is most capable. Obviously, it's not just your individual choice – all staffing decisions will be through a democratic, 'majority wins' voting process.

You will also get access to profiles of other Advance Bookers – your co-passengers – on your flight and you can send them *"Sit with me!"* requests. If someone accepts your request, you will both be assigned adjacent seats and given complimentary copies of the World Airport Codes almanac.

Before takeoff, the captain, in crisp English, will announce the seat numbers of all celebrities and tycoons on the flight. Autograph and networking events will take place once the plane reaches cruising altitude.

It will be a fantastic flight with an unlimited usage of mobile phones, pre-mixed pink wines and bathrooms with twisting faucets. Airlines would have moved beyond cross-selling sandwiches and teddy bears on flights to instead providing real value added services to the passengers strapped into their seats. Such as haircuts, shaves, manicures, teeth cleaning and root canals. Taking a cue from the revolution that my Peace Prize sparked off, governments would have abolished visas so you will breeze through immigration when you land. Lastly, cab rides from the airport to the city center would simply be one flat fare of $40; no bargaining, no ripping off and no stink bombs required. Take it or leave it.

Flying would indeed be such a pleasure.

And while we wait for the above to become reality, planes are continuing to go higher. Flights are getting safer. Travel is getting cheaper. Journeys are getting faster. In short, the world is getting smaller.

And aisle seats still remain occupied. And families continue to wait for their loved ones at Arrivals. And people always have stories to tell.

And you know, that is not really such a bad situation to be in.

So grab another book, or put on your headphones to listen to some music, or turn to your neighbor and start a conversation.

And just sit back, relax and enjoy the flight.

ENDNOTES

"People come back from flights and tell you a story like it's a horror story. They act like their flight was like a cattle car in the 1940s in Germany. That's how bad they make it sound. They're like, 'It was the worst day of my life. We didn't board for 20 minutes and they made us sit there on the runway for 40 minutes.' Oh really? What happened next? Did you fly in the air, incredibly, like a bird? Did you partake in the miracle of human flight you non-contributing zero?"

— Louis C.K.

REFERENCES AND IMAGES

In a world flooded with literary drivel, I am pleased to have contributed such a comprehensive treatise on a subject of such critical importance to mankind. This obviously needed exhaustive research and my primary source of information was the fieldwork done on the flights I have taken, sitting usually on the aisle seat. Over and above, I extensively used the internet and other sources to research related information, quotes, and draw inspiration for ideas. Anecdotes in the chapter 'What the Heck, Captain!' and elsewhere, have been adapted with some creative liberties, from various news articles.

- Operations Manuals and Standard Operating Procedures of various airlines: While I found that my television set came with a more useful instructions booklet, these gave me some perspective on what pilots and cabin crew really do while on a flight.
- www.wikipedia.org: For information on anything under the sun.
- www.skygod.com: A collection of aviation related quotes.
- www.goodreads.com: An excellent collection of quotes on all subjects.
- www.seinfeldscripts.com: Quotes from the sitcom, *Seinfeld.*
- Aeroflot says drunk pilot 'no big deal', Adrain Blomfield, *The Telegraph,* 03/02/2009
- Stuck in the Middle originally appeared as a column by the author in *BLink, Hindu Business Line,* 22/05/2015

- Aeroflot sorry for 'drunk' pilot scare, Matthew Weaver, *The Guardian,* 04/02/2009
- My face-to-face encounter with the 'drunk' Aeroflot pilot, Ira Iosebashvili, *The Guardian,* 05/02/2009
- Thissh issh your captain sshpeaking: Passengers revolt over 'drunken pilot', Graham Smith, *The Daily Mail,* 04/02/2009
- This is your pilot slurring: Garbled message from cockpit sparks passenger rebellion, Shaun Walker, *The Independent,* 04/02/2009
- Aeroflot passengers revolt on drunk pilot fears, Ben Mutzabaugh, *USA Today,* 04/02/2009
- Report on pilots who overshot airport, Matthew Wald, *The New York Times,* 16/12/2009
- Indonesia plane lands at Tabing not Padang, *BBC News,* 15/10/2012
- British Scareways, Brain Flynn, *The Sun,* 27/08/2010
- Air India passenger jet plummets 7,000 ft after co-pilot hits control stick while adjusting his seat, *Daily Mail,* 02/12/2010
- Co-pilot moved seat, sent jetliner plummeting, Brad Lendon, *CNN,* 30/11/2010
- India inquiry after Jet Airways plane drops 5,000 feet over Turkey, *BBC,* 14/08/2014
- Captain cans coughing teen from 10-hour flight, Blair Soden, *ABC News,* 28/03/2007
- 'Bye, Bye' Baby: Mother, son booted from plane, William Mara, *ABC News,* 13/07/2007
- Mother says Baby's recurring 'Bye Bye Plane' comment got them kicked off airplane, *Associated Press, Fox News,* 12/07/2007
- World discovers a new hero: The air steward who lost his cool, grabbed a beer, slid down plane's emergency chute and launched himself into stardom on Facebook, David Gardner, *Daily Mail,* 11/08/2010
- Fed-up flight attendant makes sliding exit, Andy Newman and

Ray Rivera, *The New York Times,* 09/08/2010

- Passenger kicked off Horizon Air flight for being too tall, David Parker Brown, *AOL Travel,* 01/04/2011
- Man turns violent on board Mumbai-Delhi Indigo flight; threatens, attacks crew member, Tanina Biswas and Sabyasachi Dasgupta, *NDTV,* 08/11/2012
- Property developer who went on drunken rampage on plane escapes prison, Laura Roberts, *The Telegraph,* 03/07/2010
- Drunk thug tried to open jet doors, Vince Soodin, *The Sun,* 06/07/2010
- Bizarre News: Passenger beat up by drunk air stewards, *Female First*
- Drunken flight attendants beat Aeroflot passenger, paper says, Samantha Shields, *Bloomberg.com* 21/07/2004
- 17 Scots arrested in Amsterdam after 'mini riot' on flight from Glasgow, Ruth Doherty, *AOL,* 17/12/2012
- Plane passenger woke, stood, urinated on others and went back to sleep, *The Guardian,* 12/09/2015
- Alec Baldwin thrown off AA flight at LAX for 'playing game' on phone, Erin Calabrese and David K. Li, *New York Post,* 07/12/2011
- The 7 worst things airline pilots have done mid-flight, E. Reid Ross, *Cracked.com,* 24/06/2012
- If you are not comfortable being seated in an (extremely comfortable) exit row, Neel Shah, *Esquire,* 04/09/2009
- People on planes do the weirdest things, James Durston, *CNN,* 15/12/2012
- A Mile-high Threesome originally appeared as a column by the author in *BLink, Hindu Business Line,* 15/08/2014
- Cannabis blunder at Tokyo airport, *BBC News,* 26/05/2008
- Dog misses planted drugs in Japan, customs embarrassed, *CBC News,* 26/05/2008

The cover photographs have been shot by the trendsetting Madhur Shroff (www.madhurshroff.com). It was inspired by the work of Turkish photographer and film-maker, Cansu Boguslu (www.cansuboguslu.com). Most of the stock images have been procured from 123RF Stock Photography and have been credited below.

IT ALL BEGINS AT THE AIRPORT

- Firing squad: © Fernando Cortes De Pablo/123RF.com
- Security check: © Anatoly Tiplyashin/123RF.com
- Fighting man: © wrangel/123RF.com

THE OPTIMAL BOARDING STRATEGY

- Business suits: © Dmitriy Shironosov/123RF.com
- Shoelaces: © Igor Mojzes/123RF.com

SHOULD I WINDOW OR SHOULD I AISLE?

- Clouds: © Elena Elisseeva/123RF.com
- Stewardess and steward: Photos by Madhur Shroff
- Monks: © Prissana Boonprasob/123RF.com
- Train travel: modified; © David Gilbert/123RF.com
- Rolling hills: © Angus Benham/123RF.com
- Elbow doctor: © Cathy Yeulet/123RF.com

FLIGHT SAFETY: FROM TAKEOFF TO LANDING

- Tilting plane: © Vladislav Moiseev/123RF.com
- Cow and plane: modified; © mihtiander/123RF.com and © Brian Kenney/123RF.com

- Protractor: © picsfive/123RF.com
- Water bottle: www.rgbstock.com; photograph by chidseyc (Chris)

BEYOND THE SAFETY INFORMATION CARD

- Giraffe in window: modified; © Sarunyu Glanjit/123RF.com and © Tyler Olson/123RF.com
- Gladiator: © Nejron/123RF.com
- Cycle lock: © grigvovan/123RF.com
- Mid-air piracy: modified; © Matej Hudovernik/123RF.com
- Ocean: © Sergey Nivens/123RF.com
- Skydiver: © German Skydiver/123RF.com
- Air Traffic Control: © Fernando Barozza/123RF.com

LOOS, BOOZE AND THE FOOD YOU CHOOSE

- Restroom sign: © Djordje Radivojevic/123RF.com
- Alternate restroom sign: modified; © Sabri Deniz Kizil/123RF.com
- Sultan and exotic woman: © anyka/123RF.com
- In-flight meal: © Fedor Kondratenko/123RF.com
- Lightning: © Konstantin Kamenetskiy/123RF.com
- Stadium: © Daniel Padavona/123RF.com
- Fire eater: © Nejron/123RF.com

WHAT THE HECK, CAPTAIN!

- Mannekin pis: © Chris Dorney/123RF.com
- Dhobi: © Michael Smith/123RF.com
- Drunk man: © smithore/123RF.com
- Pilots: © Andres Rodriguez/123RF.com

- Airport runway: © Josef Hanus/123RF.com
- 747 Cockpit: © Benis Arapovic/123RF.com
- Urinals: © Phalakon Jaisangat/123RF.com
- Throat: © Piotr Marcinski/123RF.com
- Witch: © krasnoyarsk/123RF.com
- Wheelchair: © Maksym Bondarchuk/123RF.com
- Cocktails: © Dmitriy Shironosov/123RF.com

AWESOME CO-PASSENGER CONVERSATIONS

- Baby on plane: © Danil Roudenko/123RF.com
- Flight crew: © Andres Rodriguez/123RF.com
- Model on airplane: © Yuri Arcurs/123RF.com
- Cheerleader: © Tangalooma Long Pasia

CLEARED TO LAND

- Busy airport: © Wisnu Haryo Yudhanto/123RF.com
- Immigration officer: © taolmor/123RF.com
- Lost luggage: © Hongqi Zhang/123RF.com
- Sniffer dog: © Monika Wisniewska/123RF.com
- Maze: © skvoor/123RF.com

PERFECT AIRPORT PICKUPS

- Taxis: © Claire Norman/123RF.com
- Protestors: © Ron Sumners/123RF.com

COMMERCE, LITERATURE AND ZEN

- Superhero: © Gino Santa Maria/123RF.com

- Microphones: © picsfive/123RF.com
- Auction: © Rob Marmion/123RF.com
- Birds: © Magdalena Yaramova/123RF.com
- Writer with quill: © anyka/123RF.com
- Spectacles: © Sergei Kleshnev/123RF.com

ACKNOWLEDGMENTS

I didn't really expect to go beyond 20 pages when I started this book or to finish it in five weeks – just nights and weekends. But well, time flies and words flow when you are having some good single malts. Let me end with some final thoughts.

All views expressed in this book are entirely my own. Neither my organization nor my family nor my friends subscribe to these, or to any of my views, now that I think of it. I am singularly unique. I claim complete and exclusive ownership of my views.

For the lawyers reading this: I have liberally used brand names of various products, services and organizations. The brands belong to their respective registered owners. I just want to clarify – I do not own any of those brands. I wish I did. But I don't.

I would like to express, on behalf of self and country, my deepest gratitude to the Nobel Committee; I am indeed blessed – that too, three times over.

To my family, friends, crushes, classmates, neighbors and ex and why colleagues – thank you for pushing me, each in your own annoying way, to finally put pen to paper.

To my doctor who I hope, given his stellar quack record, will make this book go viral.

Goo, Jags, Manish, Nikhil and Shroffy: I can search high and low, but a bigger group of skeptics I will not find.

Devika, Rajesh, Gayatri, Kunal, Clinton and Dom: Hail to the seventh floor. Your conviction so nicely compensates for the cynicism of those identified above.

A quick Whatsapp to my Social Velas group – the best panel of "know nothing in particular" experts that one can access.

A special mention of Gert, Kamran, Sarvesh, Jaya, Rahul and Ram. I really don't know who has been more fortunate – me to have such awesome gentlemen as bosses, or them to have such a kickass professional as an employee.

Anjali, Anoopa, Apoorva, Avinash, Dhiraj, Dhruv, Fareen, Gourav, Hemant, Ishan, Josy, Kunal, Madhur, Munish, Nandini, Pooja, Ram, Ravi, Sangeeta, Senthil, Srikesh, Sudha, Sunitha, Uday, Yash and Zaki: I'll be damned, you all have been most encouraging in this journey.

Maithili, Priya, Shirley and Zee: the book went from 'this is absolutely godawful' to 'it's still quite lousy' thanks to all your invaluable inputs. I owe you all big – maybe a Cessna each.

Akash, Sandhya and Vijay at Jaico – thank you for your patience and incredible partnership. And to their awesome team (Ahalya, Karishma, Lakshmi, Marina, Meera, Nita, Nityasya, Pheji), here is a misplaced, comma. And no, I won't correct it. I won't, I won't, I won't!

To the digital crackerjacks at Togglehead (Aatef, Akshay, J.D, Krish, Naitri, Nelson, Niyati and Shivani), a round of beers on me whenever you all reach legal drinking age.

And to the folks who ignored this saying it's too niche, if sales cross 5,000 copies, visualize my thumb on my nose, fingers wagging, and me going, *"Na Na Na Na Na Nyaaaaah."*

My love to my father who is nine books ahead of me and continues to find ways to amaze and inspire me. And to my mother who has, despite popular opinion, firmly believed that I am the smartest, coolest and handsomest man on earth.

My dear Reina, Rayan and Gia – may you always remain too young to read this book.

And finally, beyond the banter, I must acknowledge the resolve that is needed to maintain poise and presence of mind at 38,000 feet. It is not an easy job by any stretch and my gratitude and appreciation for the aviation industry, and its gracious men and women, who keep the skies safe and friendly for all of us. A heartfelt thank you.

I started this expecting to have a handful of copies in circulation. But maybe this will find its way to the seatback pockets of a wider audience. I will welcome feedback on aspects of air travel that I haven't covered, anecdotes that you would like to share, or anything else related, or unrelated, to flight.

You can find me at:

www.aislebedamned.com
rishi@aislebedamned.com
www.facebook.com/AisleBeDamned
@AisleBeDamned
@RishiPiparaiya

Or on some aisle seat, on some flight, to somewhere.

Godspeed.

Rishi Piparaiya
Mumbai, India (BOM)
July 2013

ABOUT THE AUTHOR

"Let the only things higher than the airplanes in the sky,
be the stories that I tell to others and the castles that
I build for myself."
— Rishi Piparaiya

Professionally, Rishi has such randomly vast experience that LinkedIn has had to set up a dedicated server to host his profile. Organization charts start from wherever he stands and he essentially does whatever the heck he feels like. Prior to this, quite like the rock-climbing Tom Cruise in MI-2, he was skillfully navigating the corporate ladder. He headed sales and marketing for a financial services multinational; a good gig where his wonderful teams did all the work and he showed up to take the credit. Before that, he spent years dozing his way up to a super duper position at a fine global bank, which ironically never sleeps. His other professional claims to fame include running football betting syndicates in Spain and setting up random Internet businesses that contributed to the dotcom bust.

Academically, he perfected the art of cracking exams without attending classes at the Cathedral & John Connon School, University of Rochester and Cornell University.

Athletically, the dude completes half marathons (21 km for the sportingly ignorant) in well under three hours. To put this speed into perspective, the rate of continental drift is four cms per year: landmasses take 500,000 years to cover the distance that he can in barely a few hours. To put this time in perspective, the Mohenjo-daro and Harappa baloney that they taught us in school is 5,000 years old. So it's no wonder that champion distance-running nations like Kenya and Ethiopia are clamoring to give him citizenship.

Physically, he is a lot more handsome than his photograph suggests. His chiseled Greek God features actually manifest themselves a lot better in oil portraits.

Financially, everything that he invests in, depreciates. He is credited with pioneering what is now widely known as the à la carte investment strategy, because it is so damned contrary to what Buffet does.

Recreationally, he enjoys texting and will be happy to communicate with you. Please use one of the following addresses, depending on the nature of your correspondence.

- Comments on the book: rishi@aislebedamned.com
- Serious stuff: rishi_piparaiya@hotmail.com
- Fan mail and racy photos: gmail@piparaiya.com

Intellectually, this is his first book.

JAICO PUBLISHING HOUSE

Elevate Your Life. Transform Your World.

ESTABLISHED IN 1946, Jaico Publishing House is home to world-transforming authors such as Sri Sri Paramahansa Yogananda, Osho, the Dalai Lama, Sri Sri Ravi Shankar, Sadhguru, Robin Sharma, Deepak Chopra, Jack Canfield, Eknath Easwaran, Devdutt Pattanaik, Khushwant Singh, John Maxwell, Brian Tracy, and Stephen Hawking.

Our late founder Mr. Jaman Shah first established Jaico as a book distribution company. Sensing that independence was around the corner, he aptly named his company Jaico ('Jai' means victory in Hindi). In order to service the significant demand for affordable books in a developing nation, Mr. Shah initiated Jaico's own publications. Jaico was India's first publisher of paperback books in the English language.

While self-help, religion and philosophy, mind/body/spirit, and business titles form the cornerstone of our non-fiction list, we publish an exciting range of travel, current affairs, biography, and popular science books as well. Our renewed focus on popular fiction is evident in our new titles by a host of fresh young talent from India and abroad. Jaico's recently established translations division translates selected English content into nine regional languages.

Jaico distributes its own titles. With its headquarters in Mumbai, Jaico has branches in Ahmedabad, Bangalore, Chennai, Delhi, Hyderabad, and Kolkata.

SINCE 1946